Online Business

Investing In Yourself - Work from Home and Earn Passive Income

Learn How to Start An Online Business For FREE:
www.lacobizonlinebusiness.com

Table of Contents

Introduction 4

Part 1: Setting Up to Run a Business Online 8

    The Quick Guide to Starting an Online Business 9

    Starting an Online Business – Is It For You? 14

    Pros and Cons of Creating a Company 18

    What Kind Of Online Business Do You Choose? 21

    How Much Startup Money Do You Need? 24

    Finding the Right Niche 26

    Let's Talk Passive Income 30

    What's Your Mindset? 38

    Why Do People Fail At Online Businesses? 41

Part 2: Choosing Your Business Model 47

    Setting up Your First Online Business 48

    Affiliate Marketing 55

    Blogging 71

    Facebook 86

    YouTube 93

    Drop Shipping 109

Learn How to Start An Online Business For FREE:
www.lacobizonlinebusiness.com

Shopify 116

Amazon FBA 126

Publishing on Amazon 134

Part 3: Running Your Business Successfully..........................139

21 Secrets to Online Business Success 140

More Mistakes to Avoid...148

Scaling Your Business 152

Motivation 156

Press Outreach – 8 Mistakes to Avoid 160

Don't Sink Your Business This Quickly..............................165

Conclusion 173

Learn How to Start An Online Business For FREE:
www.lacobizonlinebusiness.com

Introduction

I want to thank you and congratulate you for downloading the book, "Online Business: Investing In Yourself - Work from Home and Earn Passive Income."

This book contains proven steps and strategies on how to set yourself up with an online business and start bringing in a steady passive income.

You may not realize it but, every single day, more than $3 trillion changes hands. More than $650 million of that changes hands daily through Internet businesses alone and over the next 10 years or so, it is expected that three billion more people will have access to the Internet.

As more and more money is spent via Internet businesses, the opportunities for new business entrepreneurs to build up a decent income from an online business are there for the taking and there isn't any point in sitting on the sidelines, wishing you could have a slice of what is fast becoming a very lucrative pie.

Starting an online business does not need to be expensive; indeed, some businesses can be started with just a few dollars but, before you think that I am going to let you in on the secret of making money online hand over fist, without doing anything, I'm not. Listen up; you can earn serious money online BUT you must be prepared to put in the work. There is no such thing as getting something for nothing and if that is what you are looking for, think again.

What you will learn in this guide is what you need to do to set up and prepare for an online business, what types of business

Learn How to Start An Online Business For FREE:
www.lacobizonlinebusiness.com

models you can choose from as well as lots of tips on succeeding in your chosen area. Oh yeah, and quite a few mistakes that you really should avoid making if you can. If you are ready to learn how to make money with an online business, jump right in.

Thanks again for downloading this book, I hope you enjoy it!

Learn How to Start An Online Business For FREE:
www.lacobizonlinebusiness.com

© Copyright 2019 by LacoBiz - All rights reserved.

This document is geared towards providing exact and reliable information in regards to the topic and issue covered. The publication is sold with the idea that the publisher is not required to render accounting, officially permitted, or otherwise, qualified services. If advice is necessary, legal or professional, a practiced individual in the profession should be ordered.

- From a Declaration of Principles which was accepted and approved equally by a Committee of the American Bar Association and a Committee of Publishers and Associations.

In no way is it legal to reproduce, duplicate, or transmit any part of this document in either electronic means or in printed format. Recording of this publication is strictly prohibited and any storage of this document is not allowed unless with written permission from the publisher. All rights reserved.

The information provided herein is stated to be truthful and consistent, in that any liability, in terms of inattention or otherwise, by any usage or abuse of any policies, processes, or directions contained within is the solitary and utter responsibility of the recipient reader. Under no circumstances will any legal responsibility or blame be held against the publisher for any reparation, damages, or monetary loss due to the information herein, either directly or indirectly.

Respective authors own all copyrights not held by the publisher.

The information herein is offered for informational purposes solely, and is universal as so. The presentation of the information is without contract or any type of guarantee assurance.

Learn How to Start An Online Business For FREE:
www.lacobizonlinebusiness.com

The trademarks that are used are without any consent, and the publication of the trademark is without permission or backing by the trademark owner. All trademarks and brands within this book are for clarifying purposes only and are owned by the owners themselves, not affiliated with this document.

Learn How to Start An Online Business For FREE:
www.lacobizonlinebusiness.com

Part 1: Setting Up to Run a Business Online

Learn How to Start An Online Business For FREE:
www.lacobizonlinebusiness.com

The Quick Guide to Starting an Online Business

Before we delve deeper into starting your online business, here's a quick guide. Starting and running an online business is easy enough; the success is down to you and the following steps have been proven to help many entrepreneurs find their way to a decent online income:

Step One: Find a Need in the Market and Fill it

The biggest mistake that many people make is to find the product they want to sell before they find the market. Always start by looking for your market first and you do this by finding a group of people who are all looking for some solution to the same or similar problem but are struggling to find the service or the product that provides that solution. Thanks to the Internet, you can do this quite easily:

- Go to forums online and see what people are talking about, what questions are being asked and what the problems are that people are struggling to solve
- Do some keyword research; you are looking for keywords that loads of people are searching but are finding few web results
- Go to the websites of your potential competition and see what they are doing to solve the problem. Take what you learned from them and come up with something better – you know the market exists, all you have to do is sell to it, better than your competition does.

Step Two: Write Great Copy

When you write your copy, follow the formula below; it's proven to work, taking a visitor through the entire process of arriving on your website right through to making a purchase:

Learn How to Start An Online Business For FREE:
www.lacobizonlinebusiness.com

- Great headlines grab the attention
- Talk about the problem that your product or service is going to solve
- Establish your authority and credibility as a person who can solve this
- Add in a few testimonials from those who have already used the product (easier if you are an affiliate unless you have your own product that has already been sold a few times)
- Talk about this product or service and how your users are going to benefit from it
- Make readers an offer
- Give them a great guarantee
- Create a sense of urgency
- Ask them to buy – a call to action

As you write, your focus needs to be on how this product or service is unique, the only one that will solve the problem or improve life for them. Put yourself in the shoes of a customer and ask, "What will it do for me?"

Step Three: Design Your Website and Build it

Now you have your market, your product and your selling copy, its time to get that website on the go. Keep things simple but attention-grabbing; you have only a few seconds to grab the attention of your visitors otherwise they will move on. Keep these tips in mind:

- Choose a white background with a couple of good fonts
- Make sure your website is easy to navigate, on all pages
- Don't fill it up with audio, video or graphics unless it is needed for your message

Learn How to Start An Online Business For FREE: www.lacobizonlinebusiness.com

- Make sure to include an email opt-in offer so you can start building your email list (some people offer a free eBook or something to visitors to sign up)
- Make the buying process simple – two clicks or less to checkout
- Make your website user and customer friendly

Step Four – Drive Traffic

The best way to do this is using the search engines and PPC (pay per click) advertising. PPC offers two advantages – first, the ads will appear on search pages straight away and second, you can use them to test headlines, keywords, price and so on. You get traffic straight to your site immediately and they are a great tool to help you work out what your best keywords and approaches are – do monitor the results carefully. Once you have those keywords, you can use them in your copy and in your website code, boosting your search rankings significantly.

Step Five: Establish Yourself as an Expert

The Internet is used by millions of people every day to look for information. Give other websites that information for free and you search rankings will rise as will your traffic. Make sure you always include links to your website with each bit of information you share:

- Give something away for free, some content that shows your expertise. It could be an article, a video, a podcast, etc.; whichever it is, distribute it widely through social media sites and online directors;
- On the best content you publish on your website, add a link to "Send to a Friend".

Learn How to Start An Online Business For FREE:
www.lacobizonlinebusiness.com

- Find the forums in your industry, join them and become an expert. Do the same with social media sites where you know your target audience is reading. Be active on those sites otherwise your credibility will not grow

While you get a longer reach to a bigger audience you also get link backs from any site that publishes your content and search engines welcome relevant links with open arms.

Step Six: Use Email Marketing

By providing an opt-in on your website you start to build an email list and the power of this cannot be underestimated. Use that list because anyone that has signed up has told you that you can send them emails:

- You give them what they have asked you for
- You can build up long and lasting relationships
- You can measure the response
- Email marketing is a cheap way of advertising because it is targeted at people who want to hear from you

Step Seven: Use Upselling and Back-end Sales to Boost Your Income

Developing a lifetime value for each customer is a critical marketing strategy; around 35% of people who buy from you will come back and buy again but only if you keep in touch with them. The first sale is the hard part so make sure you use upselling and back-end sales to tempt them into buying again:

- Offer them a product that matches or complements what they originally bought
- Send them loyalty coupons by email for their next visit

Learn How to Start An Online Business For FREE: www.lacobizonlinebusiness.com

- When they purchase, offer related or similar products on the Thank You page

If you reward a customer for buying from you they are likely to become a loyal customer.

Things change very fast on the Internet but the principles that surround starting online businesses remain the same. Following this formula properly will help propel you to success.

Time to take a deeper look.

Learn How to Start An Online Business For FREE:
www.lacobizonlinebusiness.com

Starting an Online Business – Is It For You?

Before you get started on setting up some kind of online business you need to take the time to consider whether it is right for you or not. There are loads of benefits to starting an online business, first and foremost, the money that can be made but while that's a great motivator, don't expect to become a millionaire overnight – it won't happen. There really isn't any guarantee that you can get rich with any business, let alone one online, but you can with the right amount of work and dedication, bring in another income to boost the coffers. Of course, if you put the right work in, there is every chance that you can make a huge success of your new business and quit working for your employer.

However, money isn't the only reason. Ask 100 people why they started their own online business and you will get many answers. Some will tell you that they want personal freedom, the ability to take control of their own time and future. It means not having to work for someone else, not having to answer to another person and if you find yourself getting fed up with the daily grind, fed up with working to line someone else's pockets then starting your own business could be the thing for you.

Financial freedom is a big reason for starting your own business. While you may never be a millionaire, you can earn enough money to give yourself a better life, more control over your own money, money that goes into your bank account not someone else's. You put in the work, you reap the rewards.

Can you live the life you always wanted to live? Yes, provided that life is a realistic one. Provided you are prepared to face the challenges head-on, you can succeed. As well as or instead of the boss you work for now, you are going to gain more – the market,

Learn How to Start An Online Business For FREE:
www.lacobizonlinebusiness.com

your customers, your goals, anything and everything that affects your business will become the boss of you. Your bills are still coming in – can you make the money you need to pay them and still have a great lifestyle?

Ask yourself a few questions and you will find the answer to that question

Questions About Entrepreneurship You Need to Answer:

If you learn just one thing from all of this, it should be that critical thinking is the key to success. We all know that, when you look for information and resources on the Internet, you have to determine if what you are reading is the truth or complete BS. Believe it or not in amongst all the BS there are some real nuggets of gold to be found and one of my goals is to help you find it.

To start with, DO NOT EVER take everything you read on the Internet for granted. Analyze everything, try everything, retain what is working and chuck what isn't. You are going to meet many dead ends on your journey but, rather than letting them beat you and giving in, treat them as a learning curve and move on.

So, this critical thinking. There are three parts to it:

- Ask questions
- Ask a few more questions
- And then ask more

Start by asking yourself this question:

Learn How to Start An Online Business For FREE: www.lacobizonlinebusiness.com

What Are My Chances of Success?

Well, according to most, over 90% of all new online businesses will fail but does that mean you should give up? No. Launching any business is tough. The idea you had may be the biggest flop of the year. Your second idea may start well and then dry up. There are a lot of people out there all trying to do what you want to do; you aren't just in competition with small startups like you, you are also competing with the biggest of corporations, those that have a never-ending stack of money and resources. The likelihood is, you are going to have to try several times before success comes your way.

On the other hand, your first try might be the successful one. If you put the time in, do your research properly, set your business up the right way, there is no reason why it should fail. That 90% failure rate covers every single business you could possibly think of and there are loads of things you can do to make your chances better. Also, don't forget, with the Internet, businesses are more accessible now than they have ever been; if you have a computer/laptop, and a decent connection to the Internet, you have what you need to start that successful business.

Is This Something You Can Do While Working Full-Time Elsewhere?

Yes it is. Most startups begin as a side job. While it can be tough to hold down a full-time job and get a new business off the ground it can be done. It will mean that you have money coming in to ensure you can survive while you get going and that means less risk for you.

What about Investors?

Learn How to Start An Online Business For FREE: www.lacobizonlinebusiness.com

You don't need investors. You could go down the route of looking for external capital but, right now, it is a complication you don't need. If you use other people's money to get your business going, you will be forever worried about what happens if it doesn't work. Plus, it also means others get to interfere in what you do. Bootstrapping is the way to go and that means going it alone.

Those are the main questions you need to consider. If you are still convinced that you can do this, indeed that you want to, then read on to discover what the pros and cons are of starting your own company.

Learn How to Start An Online Business For FREE:
www.lacobizonlinebusiness.com

Pros and Cons of Creating a Company

If you want to get started on your own online business, you need to understand why you want to do it and what challenges you are likely to face as you go. We'll look now at what the pros and cons are. Read through them and ask yourself if the pros are something you want, if the cons are things you can overcome.

Pros

- **Personal Freedom**

Most of us work at least 40 hours per week to keep the money coming in and, for many, those hours are controlled by the person you work for. Start your own business and you get to control when you work, how and even why you work. Instead of wearing yourself into the ground lining someone else's pocket, do what you want to and line your own.

- **Quit Your 9-5 Job**

There aren't many people who actually enjoy going to work every day. Working to someone else's rules, working the hours they set, working to their structures. You could leave all that behind and set your own schedule, your own rules.

- **More Financial Freedom**

When you work for someone else, your finances are determined by what they pay you. Work for yourself and your finances are in your control. You earn what you want, spend what you want, provided you put the hours in and you get to set the hours. And if do put the hours in, you have the potential to make a success of your business and that means you could make more money than you ever dreamed of.

Learn How to Start An Online Business For FREE: www.lacobizonlinebusiness.com

Cons

With everything, no matter how good it seems, there are also downsides and the same goes for setting up your own company:

- **Personally Accountable**

When you work for another person, you have to go by their deadlines. That may seem like a pro to some people but it does give you a structure to work to and they do hold you accountable. Go to work for yourself and those goalposts are gone. It's down to you to provide your own motivation and your own system of accountability otherwise the only sure thing is failure.

- **More Isolated**

You may not like your job but the one thing your working environment does give you is interaction with other people. When you work for yourself, you will be spending long periods of time by yourself and you will need to make the effort to get out and meet other people.

- **Not So Stable Financially**

You may gain the financial freedom that you want but, when you first start out at the very least, your finances will not be very stable. The market is very unpredictable and you will spend quite some time wondering whether you are going to have enough money to survive. This is why many people opt to start a new business as a sideline to start with, so they have the financial stability they need along with the money to get started without worrying too much.

Learn How to Start An Online Business For FREE: www.lacobizonlinebusiness.com

Once you have weighed up the pros and cons you can move on to the next step – choosing your business.

Learn How to Start An Online Business For FREE:
www.lacobizonlinebusiness.com

What Kind Of Online Business Do You Choose?

Pretty much every day, someone, somewhere says that they want to start their own business but they don't know what they would do. This is one of the biggest sticking points and the way around it is to look at all your options, noting down what skills you are strong in and having a brainstorming session, either with yourself or a trusted friend, on ways that you could monetize several different models.

Before you start to even think about the niche you want to get involved in, you need to decide what kind of business you are going to start and, as you go through each of the business types, try to think of ideas for each one where you can answer yes to each of these questions:

- Is it an idea you care about?
- Does this idea fulfill a need?
- Can the people who would potentially be interested in the idea be able to afford it?
- Can you make yourself and your idea different from all your other competitors, i.e. do you have a unique angle?

Now we'll look at each business type in turn.

Physical Products

The idea here would be to set up an online e-commerce store selling physical products. This can be done from a digital store to remove the barriers between you and a physical store, to offer your customers the convenience of shopping online and selection. Starting a store could be as simple as setting up a Shopify account or setting up your own website to sell your

Learn How to Start An Online Business For FREE:
www.Iacobizonlinebusiness.com

goods from and, depending on how well your business does, how easily you can scale it, you could be rolling in money. The cost of setting up will depend on the route you take but it can be done for just a few dollars per month. There are two ways to do this too – you can either produce your own products, in which case you need to consider production and storage costs, or you could choose affiliate marketing where you promote goods for other people. We'll discuss that in Part 2.

Digital Products

Not everything you sell has to be physical. You could offer eBooks or online courses for sale and these do prove to be successful sellers. The only limit here is your own creativity and, in all honesty, digital products tend to be easier to create and sell than physical products do. You don't need to take materials, stock, suppliers, or shipping into account because everything is done online.

You could set up a membership site where people pay a monthly subscription for the digital product you provide and, done right this can be quite an easy way to make some money. It's a guaranteed source of income but only for as long as you continue to provide your customers with the value they want. And this kind of product usually works better when you offer something for free too as this establishes you and your authority in the minds of your customers and tells them what kind of value you are offering. The real costs here are in setting up a website and running it, creating the product if you opt to outsource and the cost of the membership site.

SaaS – Software as a Service

Learn How to Start An Online Business For FREE:
www.lacobizonlinebusiness.com

Software has long been a massive industry and it will continue to be so but, instead of offering a software package as a one-off sale, consider SaaS. With this, the application software gets hosted on your server and you charge a monthly subscription fee to access it. However, this is not cheap to start up because of the investment needed to create that software to start with but it can be the most financially rewarding.

Coaching and Consulting

If you have a lot of expertise in a specific area, you can offer it through coaching and/or consultancy services. You can use a telephone or Skype to offer this and you can also offer it as a service or a course on your website. You would need to set an hourly fee, a per-session fee, or, if offered via the website, a membership fee. You do need to consider everything you need to run that business, such as setting up the website and so on and factor it all into the cost of starting up.

Services

Perhaps you have some kind of skill that you could offer to others. Services such as writing, graphic design, website building, editing and so on are all types of services that you could offer on a freelance basis. You do need to put a lot of work into it though, ensure you make the right connections and find the people that are going to pay for the services you offer. This will cost you, pretty much, the setup and running costs of a website although you may need to consider any additional materials you might need as your business grows.

Learn How to Start An Online Business For FREE:
www.lacobizonlinebusiness.com

How Much Startup Money Do You Need?

So, you've got all these ideas floating around in your head and you are champing at the bit to get going. But, there is one question you need to be able to answer – can you afford to start this business?

For many online businesses, the startup costs are actually quite low but you will need to consider these questions:

Do I Need To Get Funding?

Should you even consider approaching an investor or taking out a bank loan to finance your new business? The big plus to doing so is that you have money to get going with and that means you can get off and running faster. However, if you opt to take an investor on board you lose a certain amount of control over your business and if you go down the route of taking out a loan, you need to be able to guarantee enough money to pay it back.

You could consider crowdfunding. This means raising money through future customers, offering a service or product to people prepared to pay a small contribution to get your business off the ground. Crowdfunding is a good way of making sure that your business idea is workable. However, less than 50% of crowdfunding campaigns ever succeed so you must do plenty of research if you opt to go down this route.

However, the likelihood of you needing external funding is very slim. You really don't need it to get an online business off the ground unless you opt for SaaS or development of a physical product. Most entrepreneurs wait and see if a business is going to be successful before they even think about external funding and can also provide to an outside investor that they can make the money.

Learn How to Start An Online Business For FREE: www.lacobizonlinebusiness.com

The alternative is this – stick with the money you have and launch your business that way. Build it up slowly; you don't need too much money to do this and you can always start it as a sideline and see how it goes. As money comes in, consider reinvesting a certain percentage of it back to the company as this will create a cycle of continuous growth. This is called bootstrapping and is the main way that most online businesses start.

How Much Can I Make?

How long is a piece of string? There is no way of predicting your revenue for the first few months, even year or so of your business. Some people will be making significant amounts of money fairly quickly while others will struggle for a long time. You can, however, take a guess (an educated one). Once you have picked your model, decided how you will be making money from it and chosen your niche (more about that next) you can get a rough idea of what you might make.

There really isn't any way to determine your income until your business has been up and running for a while and you have figures to work with. Only time will tell if a business is going to be successful or not so it is important to stick at it – don't throw the towel in after a week or two, things take longer than that to work.

Learn How to Start An Online Business For FREE:
www.lacobizonlinebusiness.com

Finding the Right Niche

Perhaps the most important part of your new online business lies in choosing the right niche. You want one that works, one that is sustainable and profitable and, as a new business owner this is your opportunity to pick something that you love (so long as it works) and build on it while making some money. Passion is one of the most important factors in choosing a niche especially when it looks like tough going and the money doesn't seem to be rolling in as quickly as you would like. Even if success does come, if you have no real interest in your business, your subject then you really want to enjoy it and will be less likely to put the effort in.

In essence, the niche you choose will determine which industry you will be operating in and what services and/or products you will be selling. At the end of the day, it's what you will become known for selling and choosing the right one and sticking with it is absolutely vital. First off, you are going to be facing stiff competition so specializing in better than choosing a wider variety. Second, the most important thing about online businesses is loyalty. If your customers are able to recognize you and will know exactly what you are going to be offering they are more likely to come back for more purchases. Finally, choosing a niche will help you keep your sanity and be more successful as you know exactly where your focus will be.

Choosing a Niche

The options are truly endless but don't be tempted to pick the first one you see, the one that looks the easiest or the one that looks like it will be more profitable. You need to spend a considerable amount of time analyzing your choices and narrowing them down. And you must have a set of criteria that

Learn How to Start An Online Business For FREE:
www.lacobizonlinebusiness.com

your chosen niche satisfies otherwise it's all a complete waste of time and money.

Before you choose your niche, ask yourself a few questions and write the answers down. Be completely honest with yourself because, if you want true success, you need to put your heart and soul into this.

What are my passions? Do you find yourself looking up particular subjects just for fun? Do you have any particular interests that you like to look up and get into when your workday is over? If you had the money, what would you be doing with your days, what would your idea business be?

What comes naturally to me? Do you have any specialized training in anything? Do people come to you for advice on anything in particular because you know about it? How long could it take you to become a true authority in that subject?

What do I make time for in my life? Do you have any particular hobbies or pastimes that you get involved in? Do you do any volunteer work? Anything that you do that you could turn into a business.

Have I spotted any gaps in the market? When you do research, whether it is for fun or for work, have you found information missing on certain things, information that you could provide? Is there a service or a product that would solve a problem, not just for you but for others?

Now you have the answers to those questions, you can move on.

Evaluating Ideas

Learn How to Start An Online Business For FREE: www.lacobizonlinebusiness.com

With your list of hobbies, pastimes, and other subjects that you are passionate about, you need to put each one through the following criteria. Be very thorough here because these are the absolute strongest measures of the potential success of any business. Go through your whole list and narrow it down to one or two ideas that contain a combination of real passion and decent profitability.

Google Search – You are looking for keywords that are related to the niche – single words and phrases. For example, let's say that you were knowledgeable about dog grooming; you research terms would be something along the lines of "dog grooming", "dog grooming kit", "dog grooming tutorials", and so on. You could also have "dog grooming videos", "dog grooming tips", "dog grooming books". Etc. Drill this down, get as specific as you can. What you want to do here is find the content that already exists and see what the demand is for each of your niches. Have a look at the blogs, websites and digital stores that are selling in these niches. Look at what kind of products they sell or promote. What are the blogs talking about? Who look like the leading retailers and influencers in your niches? Have a look on Pinterest, YouTube and other major social media sites. You will need to use best judgment and there is no magic formula. You will see straight away though if your proposed niche has little to no search activity. Don't discount a niche just because there is a lot of competition either; competition is prerequisite for business because it shows that there is a good demand – the hard work is done and the road has been paved. All you need to do is be a little bit different and unique.

Keyword Searches – using the terms you used in the Google searches you now need to run keyword searches. Google AdWords has a free keyword search tool provided you have an

Learn How to Start An Online Business For FREE:
www.lacobizonlinebusiness.com

account with them. Other than that, there are plenty of good ones to be found on the Internet. What you are looking for is an idea of how much search activity is around each keyword or key phrase. The higher the number, the better the activity in that niche and the more likely you are to find customers. This is a very important step; over 30% of online buyers will use Google as their starting point.

Amazon Search – it would be remiss of you not to look through the largest online marketplace in the world. While Google may be a starting point, Amazon is the most popular place for online shoppers and more than 50% of online buyers will go there first. Amazon offers a huge variety of products with good prices and plenty of verified reviews. Use your search terms from earlier plus any more that you can think of, and see what kind of products come up. How many different types are there? Are there books and/or videos on the subject? What do the reviews seem to say about the products? If a search term throws up at least five pages of results then you are looking in the right direction. This will also tell you what sort of competition you may be facing too.

Affiliate Marketing Search – look on all the top affiliate marketing network sites, like ShareASale and Clickbank, to see what products match your niche. These also give you an idea of whether there is sufficient market readiness. If two or more affiliate networks align with your niche that is a great sign. You may not opt to go down the affiliate marketing route but you can still get some great market data for the niche you want to specialize in. Plus, when your business is up and running you can always turn to affiliate marketing for extra income.

Learn How to Start An Online Business For FREE:
www.lacobizonlinebusiness.com

This is not going to be an easy part of starting an online business but it is the most important and you must spend enough time on it. If the niche you really want to get into doesn't pan out for some reason, don't give up. Pick another that you know you can get interested in and do it all over again. Do NOT rush this.

If none of your niche ideas pan out, don't worry. There are thousands to choose from and it is a very common misconception that finding one idea is the key to success. Most entrepreneurs end up scrapping their first few ideas and moving in a new direction. For example, if your favored niche of dog grooming was simply too fierce in competition for selling products, you could consider starting a blog on the subject, producing a few videos, an eBook, even using affiliate marketing. The possibilities are never-ending.

You want to be at the crossroads of profit and passion if you can and the one question you need to ask is this – can you come up with something better than is already there? Something unique, something that fills a market gap. If you can garner enough passion, excitement and interest in one niche that has enough demand, you can be well on the way to success.

Let's Talk Passive Income

If you have ever read a book called "The Four Hour Work Week" by Tim Ferriss, then there is a good chance you subscribe to the idea that if you can get a passive income going, you can do pretty much whatever you want with your life. Well, that is only true if your passive income can bring you more money than you ever needed; the hard part is in finding the ideas that work and

Learn How to Start An Online Business For FREE:
www.lacobizonlinebusiness.com

getting them to the stage where the money is coming in without you having to bat an eyelid.

Run a Google search right now and I guarantee you will see thousands of websites that tell you how to create a passive income. Some of these are good sites and others are nothing more than scams. For people who are new to online business, who want a quick income, it can be very easy to fall prey to some of these but, before you do, you need to take a big step back and understand exactly what passive income is and how it works.

Active or Passive?

Income falls into two categories – active and passive

- **Active Income**

Active income is what you are most likely doing now – working for someone else and getting paid for the 'pleasure' of doing so. You do a job and you get paid for it – once. Any regular job that you do, be it a job that pays you a salary or freelance work, your income is classed as active because you have to do something to earn it. You trade your time, effort and experience for a financial reward.

- **Passive Income**

Passive income is quite different. Instead of being paid one single time for what you do, you create value or something that brings in money in an indefinite stream. The absolute simplest way of giving you an example is a top-notch author like Stephen King. More than 40 years ago, King sat down and wrote a book called The Shining. It took him a few months but it became a bestseller and today he is still earning money from that book every time a copy of it sells.

Learn How to Start An Online Business For FREE: www.lacobizonlinebusiness.com

How to Earn a Passive Income

I'm not saying you should sit down and pen a best seller although, if you can, you should. With the advent of the Internet, there are more ways than ever to earn a passive income. You could produce and sell products or services, you could get involved in affiliate marketing and you could use adverts to bring in revenue. Even investing the traditional ay can bring in a passive income.

Here's a couple of ideas, hypothetical examples that will give you some idea of what the possibilities are and, in part 2, I'll go over several business models that can also bring you int hat passive income.

Developing a WordPress Theme

Let's say that Simon sits down and take a couple of months to come up with a fantastic theme for WordPress. It's so easy to use that anyone could use it on their WordPress site. He releases it through WordPress or through an external theme marketplace and he sits back and waits.

A customer goes looking for a fantastic theme for their site and a Google search brings up Simon's theme. The customer purchases it and the money goes to Simon. This can happen over and over again; every tie that theme is sold, Simon gets paid and he only had to do the initial work. The rest of the money coming in is passive income.

Writing a Travel Blog

Anna is a travel writer. She loves to go off on her travels around the world and tell her blog readers of all her experiences. Every

Learn How to Start An Online Business For FREE: www.lacobizonlinebusiness.com

time she goes somewhere new, she writes on her blog. How is she making money? In a few ways.

First, she has ads down the sidebar of her blog. For every click from a unique visitor, Anna gets a small amount of money. She also takes part in an affiliate program for Airbnb; this allows her to give her readers a discount code and, when any of her readers use it to book a room, she gets a percentage. Lastly, because she has done a lot of traveling, she has gotten to know many areas very well. So she writes short eBooks, city guides, that sort of thing. When anyone purchases one of these books, priced at just $5, through her website, all the money is hers to keep.

Manufacturers

Liz and Jeff also like traveling but they discovered that there is no travel bag that suits all their requirements. Instead of kicking off about it, they took matters into their own hands and they made one. They used a crowdfunding site called Kickstarter to advertise their bag and they received enough money to go into production and begin selling their bag online, Instead of having to cope with all the handling and shipping they use a fulfillment service; the bags go from manufacturing straight to the fulfillment service and Liz and Jeff don't even see them. Now they have money coming in without having to do anything and they can enjoy their travels even more.

Living the Dream

So, you can see why people love the idea of passive income; it sounds great doesn't it. In theory, you do the work once and you get paid indefinitely. Going back to our earlier example of The Shining by Stephen King. Even when he dies, his family will still make money from that book.

Learn How to Start An Online Business For FREE:
www.Iacobizonlinebusiness.com

There are other things in favor of passive income too. The work is all done up front – you write a book and that's it. Unless it needs revising you only need to write it once. And because passive income pays of work you have already done once, you can get on with other things in life. If you do decide to write a book, you can do it from anywhere. You don't have to go to an office and work 9 to 5; you can sit in your backyard in the sun and do it if you want. And once it's done you can sit back and, hopefully, reap the rewards, no matter where you are or what you are doing.

But that's not the whole story.

The Other Side of the Coin

There is no lie in what passive income can do for you but it isn't the whole truth. Yes it is perfectly possible to get paid indefinitely for something you did once but there is more to it.

Let's say that you decide you want to write posts on a blog. You could set up your own blog, keep it updated and use something like Google AdSense to bring money in passively through ads but that is going to make you minuscule amounts of cash. A better way would be to write guest posts for another leading authority site; many of these pay you a decent amount of money to write these posts and you only need to come up with a couple to keep the money rolling in.

The same is true of many of the passive income sources. You may be able to earn an indefinite payday but it won't be a big one. You may pay $10 for a copy of The Shining online but Stephen King doesn't get that; he gets less than $1 for every sale.

Learn How to Start An Online Business For FREE:
www.lacobizonlinebusiness.com

This is why many attempts at passive income fail. It takes time to pen a best selling book or design and develop a WordPress theme and, at the end of it all there is no guarantee that anyone will buy it.

For every bestselling author, there are thousands more trying to make money form a book that never sells. Thousands of people have written travel blogs but very few actually make any money from them. Books must be promoted, blogs must be kept updated constantly and themes must be kept updated and so on. So the real truth about passive income is this – it is highly unlikely that you will make enough to live on without lifting a finger; it still requires work.

The Real Truth

Now, I'm not saying that you can't make a passive income but you need to understand that it isn't straightforward – anyone who tells you that you can make a 6-figure income while you sleep is lying and is trying to scam you. You have to understand the work involved behind the scenes.

You can earn a passive income provided you put the time and the effort in and, for many people, when they weight up that time and effort against the rewards, they would actually be better off working for an active income. That isn't the case for everyone though and to dismiss passive income out of hand just because it requires work would be daft; just as daft as it is to jump in with both eyes shut because someone told you could earn money without lifting a finger.

You do not need to decide between earning a passive income and an active income. You can do both at the same time. For example:

Learn How to Start An Online Business For FREE:
www.lacobizonlinebusiness.com

If you are a website designer and you get paid an active income, you could get involved with a hosting reseller account and host their websites for a fee each month – passive income

If you take wedding photos as an active income, you can sell presets on an online marketplace for a passive income

Whatever you do for an active income you can usually find something that makes a passive income at the same time and that's a win-win situation.

Getting Started

If you are getting ready to explore the possibilities of running an online business then you definitely need to consider ways to bring in a passive income too. It may not work but, on the other hand, you may find that you can bring a few extra dollars every month. Some people have been so successful at generating passive income that it is now their main income.

Obviously, you need to have an idea for a business then you need to sit down and work out how that idea could be turned into passive income. Will you use affiliate programs? Ad networks? YouTube videos? Create a product and sell it? It really comes down to what you want to do and just how creative you can be.

Passive income is definitely real; it just may not be quite as passive as you thought it would be. You do still need to put int the work; although most of it will be upfront work, there is still stuff that needs to be done on an ongoing basis if you want a proper income.

Like anything, while it has its benefits, they don't come without a trade-off somewhere along the line. You may be able to work
Learn How to Start An Online Business For FREE:
www.lacobizonlinebusiness.com

from wherever you choose but you shouldn't bank on a significant income. Be prepared to put the work in and it may just pay off for you.

Before we move on to the business models, I want to take some time to discuss having the right mindset and how you can avoid failure in your business venture.

Learn How to Start An Online Business For FREE:
www.lacobizonlinebusiness.com

What's Your Mindset?

No matter what job you do, you must be in a certain kind of mindset to do it. Setting up an online business is no different but it requires a completely different kind of mindset. If you want your new business to be successful, whether it is your sole business r you are doing it on the side while working for someone else, you must change the way you think about things – your goals, people, achievements and money. If you don't, you are going to face many challenges that you just can't beat.

So, how do you change your mindset? What do you need to do to be successful at running an online business?

- **You Cannot Avoid Risk So Be Prepared To Take One**

Everything you do in life comes with a certain amount of risk but being prepared to actively take a risk is the first and most important mindset rule of running a business. You don't need to have much money but you do need to remove fear and be ready to take a leap into the unknown. Always build your strategy, always create a plan but never procrastinate over it all. You must be prepared to take risks, but only risks that you have carefully calculated. If you think too much you will always find a negative reason not to continue. Action comes first because, until you take the step to get that business off the ground, everything else is only in your mind.

- **Think Positively**

When you work for someone else, it is easy to get into a pattern of negative thinking, be it about your job, your boss or your colleagues. This is not a healthy thing when you start your own business. Positive thinking is key to success so don't spend too

Learn How to Start An Online Business For FREE: www.lacobizonlinebusiness.com

much time worrying over problems; instead, look for the solutions. Fix what you can and keep an optimistic view of everything.

- **Be Patient**

You won't get success five minutes after you start your new business so you need to practice patience. You want a minimum of six months before you even start to think about results and those six months are going to be all about hard work and learning. Do not put yourself under so much pressure that your creativity and innovative ideas are killed off though.

- **Be Consistent**

Whatever you have to do to get your business off the ground, be prepared to keep on repeating it. If you need to send email newsletters, do it consistently. Create content, list your products, everything must be done consistently and regularly. It's no good writing one blog post and then expecting the riches to come in – be prepared to work. Consistency gives more people the chance to start connecting with you and growing your business.

- **Stop Thinking Like a Consumer**

While you are in a steady job with a steady income, you can easily be a consumer. When you start your own business, you cannot. Consumers are focused on spending money; you need to focus on making it. Always think at least three times before you make any purchase – is it going to help your business? If not, don't buy it.

- **Network, Network, Network Some More**

Learn How to Start An Online Business For FREE: www.lacobizonlinebusiness.com

39

This is the real key to success at an online business – connecting with people who can help you grow Most likely, those closest to you won't really understand what you are trying to achieve but there are millions of people out there all trying to do the same thing and they will understand. Head to social media, online events and so on to try finding these people. Connect with them, join forums and talk with them; it's amazing how much you can learn just by chatting with someone in the same position as you and if you can get together with people that have been there and done it, you can learn from them too. The ideas will start flowing and your mind will be more open to new ideas.

The easy part about any online business is starting it; keeping it going successfully is the hard part. By changing your mindset you can be ready to start your business and be successful at it; don't leave it too late though – it's more difficult to change your mindset halfway through a job!

Learn How to Start An Online Business For FREE:
www.lacobizonlinebusiness.com

Why Do People Fail At Online Businesses?

Every day, millions of people haul themselves out of bed, get themselves ready and head out to a job in a brick and mortar business. Many of them are likely thinking that there has to be an easier way to put money in their pockets. Some of them will even know of someone who has done it, quit their job and gone it alone, setting up their own business from the warmth and comfort of home.

This sounds like a fantastic solution but most people who try it are simply not prepared. We hear time and time again of people, unhappy in their jobs, just quitting and diving straight into the very first online business solution (usually marketing) that they see. They do not prepare, they don't know anything about the business they are entering, and they have little knowledge of what they are doing and absolutely no hope of succeeding. The only option they have is to fail and sadly, most of them are not aware of it.

An astounding 90%+ of all new online businesses fail within three months but this statistic seems to be ignored by too many people who follow the same path. Why is it ignored? Why don't people take note of the failure rate? Here's why:

- Most people are blissfully unaware of the statistical probabilities they are facing

- Most people don't count themselves in that 90% so they jump blindly in

- Many find themselves talked into or reeled in by the promise of great riches into something they are totally unprepared to face

Learn How to Start An Online Business For FREE:
www.lacobizonlinebusiness.com

- Most do not heed one basic tenant – "if fail to plan, you plan to fail".

Now, I am not telling you this as a way of telling you that you are going to fail. There is always a possibility of success but it docsn't happen by magic or by accident. Succeeding at an online business comes down to a number of very important things – successful people make it a point of learning all they can about the business they are entering BEFORE they enter it. They learn how it all works, what the pros are and the cons. They learn what challenges lie ahead of them and, perhaps most importantly, they do not go into it with the expectation of becoming a millionaire overnight.

Strangely, the people who steer clear of starting a business in the real world, because they don't think they have the business acumen to do it, are all too happy to dive into an Internet business, despite not having that business acumen. For many people, the idea of an Internet business is that they don't have to drag themselves out of bed, out of the house and into work every day. They have this strange belief that they can work as and when they want, if they want, and still make a fortune. They do not seem to understand that any business, be it brick and mortar or online, requires hard work and very long hours.

The Wrong Ideas

When you look into that 90% failure rate, you can see it isn't all that surprising given the kinds of people starting these online businesses. It seems that most think all they have to do is get a website, buy a domain name and off they go. They really couldn't be further from the truth.

Learn How to Start An Online Business For FREE:
www.lacobizonlinebusiness.com

The first thing that every person looking to start an online business must have is self-discipline. People read the stories on the Internet of get-rich-quick schemes and think that they can work an hour or two a day and haul in huge riches. They don't understand why their newly built website isn't throbbing with traffic and their products are not flying off the shelf straight away. Why isn't their bank account bulging within a few days or weeks?

The second thing is that no business can be set to auto-pilot and left alone, And yes, there are businesses on the Internet where the owners no longer have to work every hour god sends but that's because they did work those hours for many hours, weeks, months, even years, to get their business built.

Third, you need to understand that nothing happens overnight and many people simply aren't prepared for the amount of time they have to invest in building a successful Internet business.

Fourth, where is their business background or acumen? They don't have it. Every business, no matter the size and no matter whether it is online or physical, will have the exact same two things in common – they are businesses and they must be run as businesses. Any business person must learn and accept that there are certain business practices to work by.

These are not hard concepts to understand. Over-heads and expenditure must be acceptable as far as projected income goes. You need to have a basic understanding of profit and loss and what each is made up of. You don't need an accountancy degree to do this but you do need a little knowledge. Let's face it, if you are one of those people who struggle to balance their checkbook at the end of the month then what hope have you got of balancing an entire business?

Learn How to Start An Online Business For FREE:
www.lacobizonlinebusiness.com

You could go down the route of hiring a tax representative; they'll let you know WHEN your tax deposits need to be made but they won't tell you IF you have to make one. They can let you know if you made a profit but they can't tell you how you made it.

Every successful business gets there through hard work, knowledge, and following the basic principles of running a business. You can't even expect a decent profit for the first few months and having enough resources, or capital, put by to see you through, from startup to your own needs, is vital. There is no substitute for this and if you don't have it, there is little point in starting a business from scratch, at least not by quitting your job. Obviously, if you intend to keep your day job for a while and work your new business as a sideline then go for it but you still need that knowledge!

Lastly, most people are not in the right mindset to succeed. We talked about mindset earlier; if you don't have the right attitude towards your business, you are guaranteed to fail. Let's look at a few of those wrong attitudes and how they lead to failure:

- **I can work as and when I want.** No, no, no! Absolutely not. You can't just decide that you are only going to work an hour a day or you can't be bothered to work today. Be prepared for long, tedious hours of working if you want any success out of your online business.

- **I can make my fortune quickly.** There is no such thing as a get-rich-quick scheme, no matter how many websites you look at that promise you instant riches. The only people getting rich out of those are the people selling you the useless information. Wealth comes with hard

Learn How to Start An Online Business For FREE: www.lacobizonlinebusiness.com

- **Who needs a business plan?** You do. Any business needs a plan just to survive and Internet businesses are no exception. The principles of a physical business apply just as much to an online business and that plan must be based on research and on sound principles.

- **Internet businesses don't have bosses.** They do – you. Where you had someone looking over your shoulder before, giving you deadlines and making sure your work was done, that's now down to you. It's up to you to make sure that you meet your deadlines and that you get everything done that needs to be done. You must set your own schedule now, your own goals and trust me when I say, if you don't do it, you might as well throw the towel in straight away and start looking for another job.

How to Avoid Failure

I've told you why people fail at online business so now I'm going to tell you how to avoid that failure. First and foremost, no business is guaranteed to succeed. Even the largest of businesses fall apart at the seams and fail in new ventures but there are ways to enhance your chances of success:

- Make that business plan and make sure you do it before you jump right into your new business. Success requires careful planning and it's down to you to list down every step that needs to be taken to get you there. Make sure you include estimates of cost and time in that plan too.

Learn How to Start An Online Business For FREE:
www.lacobizonlinebusiness.com

- You don't get anything for nothing and, while you may not be investing a lot of money, you will need to invest a lot of time. Nothing is easy but there is always a solution to a problem. Every step you take will require a certain amount of hard work, patience and time. Not everything will go as it should first time out but if you are willing to put the work in, you can succeed – you just may have to try a few times.

- Please, please, don't fall for any of the get-rich-quick schemes you see. Don't be one of those people who just line other people's pockets with their hard-earned cash. There really isn't any such thing and I can't stress that enough.

- Keep the 90% failure rate in mind and keep yourself out of it. Make sure you are in the 10% by putting in the work and the time. Be prepared to do whatever you have to do for as long as you need to do it.

Learn How to Start An Online Business For FREE:
www.lacobizonlinebusiness.com

Part 2: Choosing Your Business Model

Learn How to Start An Online Business For FREE:
www.lacobizonlinebusiness.com

Setting up Your First Online Business

Before you start considering your business model, I want to sidetrack for a minute and walk you through setting up your first business. If you take this step now, you have made a commitment to continuing. We've already been through mindset, how not to fail, passive income and general how to get yourself set up to start a business – now you need to take that next step. For most business models, you will need a website so you may as well set one up now.

Your Business Name

I'm not going to go too far on this because this is something that you should not spend too much time on. There are three things to take into account when you are choosing a name for your business:

The name should be self-explanatory if you are in a settled niche or something quite ambiguous if your niche changes fast.

Be very careful not to violate any trademarks. You might think your name is 100% unique but you do need to check first – if you don't it might cost you dearly down the line

Make your name memorable, not to long and easy to spell.

Domain Names and Web Hosting

To get a website running you will need the following three things:

- **Domain name** – the address in the web browser that takes people to your website

Learn How to Start An Online Business For FREE: www.lacobizonlinebusiness.com

- **Web Hosting** – the space on the web where your website files are uploaded. When your website is accessed all the pages come from this space via your web host.

- **CMS** – a content management system is important – instead of coding every individual page on your site, using a CMS allows you to change the design and add new pages without needing to code. The WordPress CMS is free and is also one of the best and easiest to use.

You have a choice – you can either do all three of these separately or you can choose a reputable web host that offers all three, the easiest option.

Choosing a Web Host

A good web host offers speed, security and support, as well as scalability, an important factor in growing your business and changing as your customer needs change. A hosting service can cost anything from just a few dollars to hundreds of dollars of every month. For the small business just getting off the ground, you could choose a virtual private server, cloud or managed service for as little as $10 a month up to about $100. But how do you know which web hosting provider to choose? By considering these factors when you start looking:

- **Customer Service** – how much help do you think you will need? With a basic customer support system you will get phone, email and ticket support but the turnaround times for requests will be different for each host. Some will have 24-hour support, others may offer an online chat service. Decide what level of support you are going to need and factor this into your decision.

Learn How to Start An Online Business For FREE:
www.lacobizonlinebusiness.com

- **Managed Service** – if you prefer to defer management of your website then you need to look at managed services. The provider will ensure that your website is properly configured, monitor security, provide software patches and backup your content, among other things.

- **Levels of Traffic** – you need to think about how much traffic you expect to get to your website being completely honest, because most hosts will use bandwidth use and storage to determine their charges. Bandwidth is a measure of bytes served over any specific period and if you only expect a low amount of visitors, this will also be low. Find yourself in the top spot on a Google search however, and you could be inundated. If your website is only a small one that provides to local customers you may never go over the limits in your plan but be aware; if your website is one that will put low-end servers under stress you need to pick the right server.

- **Server Type - shared** servers offer the cheapest hosting and one server box can potentially run many websites. How your website performs depends entirely on the server load coming from the other websites and you also limited in access to the capabilities of the server, only being able to upload files using SFTP or FTP. That means you don't get any shell access and you are restricted in what can be run on the server and how much access your website has to the database.

  Virtual private servers are the next level up. These are entire virtual machine instances (simulated computers) that run on a server box and, while most providers will run several n a single box, the performance tends to be

Learn How to Start An Online Business For FREE:
www.lacobizonlinebusiness.com

better than the shared hosting. You do need to have some experience with basic server management and maintenance.

If you prefer not to share performance then think about a dedicated server, one physical box that you and you alone rent. It's much the same as having the server physically sat on your desk except it is in a data center provided by the hosting provider. However, you should only consider this if you have skills in system management.

Lastly and perhaps the best choice is the cloud server. It goes without saying that these run in huge public clouds and two of the best examples are Microsoft Azure and Amazon Web Services. The providers can build the configuration that will suit your requirements and the biggest benefit is that cloud servers offer the chance for seamless scaling. If you do get a big traffic surge to your website, you just pay a little more money to handle it – no need to move or rebuild your website.

Other things to take into consideration are:

- **Unlimited Offers** - be wary. You will come across hosting providers that offer you an unlimited amount of bandwidth and storage for just a couple of dollars per month. This is not the good deal you might think it is because you really do only get what you pay for. Make sure you read the terms and conditions because, if you are only paying a couple of dollars a month there will likely be something written in that lets your provider keep your performance low or, after a specified usage level, they may even shut you down – not good for business!

Learn How to Start An Online Business For FREE:
www.Iacobizonlinebusiness.com

- **CMS** – you should opt for a portable CMS (content management system) so you are not locked in. Anything has the potential to change your web hosting plan and the last thing you want is your website locked into a specific host. Also make sure you have a backup in place for your own security.

  Open source content management systems are best and many people opt for WordPress on PHP because it will run on pretty much anything. You must update regularly and back up your site regularly so you will always be able to access your structure, media, data and content.

- **Domain Name** – all businesses, small and large should own their domain name so they can move to a different provider if needs be. Be aware that some domain name providers and web hosts will only rent you a name – if you want to move providers you would need to change it. Pay the extra and buy it outright.

That covers the basics of getting your website onto the Internet – obviously, when you choose a host, you will need to set it all up but most reputable hosts walk you through step by step and it's pretty easy.

Business Logo

You do need one of these but, unless you are a designer and can use something like Adobe Photoshop to create one, you would need to consider looking at other options:

- **99Designs** – if money is no object then this is a good idea. You pay $300 and 30 designers will each design a logo based on what information you provide. You choose

Learn How to Start An Online Business For FREE:
www.lacobizonlinebusiness.com

the best one and that designer wins the majority of the $300 you paid.

- **Freelance** – there are several freelance websites where you can pay a designer to come up with your website log. You can pay anything from $10 to $250-300, depending on what you want.

- **Fiverr** – this is ideal if you just want something quick and easy. It costs just $5 to get your logo designed but don't expect anything special.

Social Media

If you don't have social media profiles for your business set up, now is a good time to get it done. The most popular ones that business owners opt for are:

- Facebook
- Twitter
- LinkedIn
- Google+
- YouTube
- Pinterest

Pick a couple and get them set up; you don't need to add your logo, company details and any content just yet. Be wary of setting up a profile in every one of those above – each one requires monitoring and updating, not to mention interaction with followers and you will only have so much time to spare. You

Learn How to Start An Online Business For FREE:
www.lacobizonlinebusiness.com

can always add more profiles later on when you see how things go.

PayPal

It doesn't matter which method you choose for monetizing your business; the best way to get paid is using PayPal – most people prefer it because it is more secure than having to input credit card details on a website. Open a PayPal business account if you don't have one – PayPal provide full instructions on how to do this. They operate by taking a small percentage from each transaction so the account itself should be free to set up.

Google Analytics

Google Analytics is a great tool for monitoring the performance of your website as well as seeing exactly what your visitors are looking at, right do to what they do on any given page. You can see what works, what doesn't and decide what needs to be changed or ditched. It is free to install so go ahead and set it up by going to analytics.google.com. Even if you don't expect much traffic to start with, it's still worth having set up. Don't forget to add your website to it. You will be provided with a small code snippet that needs to be added to the header in your website (your host and website builder will provide instructions on how to do this) and, once done, Google Analytics will start pulling in data.

Let's move onto looking at some of the business models you can choose.

Learn How to Start An Online Business For FREE:
www.lacobizonlinebusiness.com

Affiliate Marketing

Most of you will have heard of affiliate marketing but do you know what it is? It is perhaps one of the oldest of all the marketing practices in the world, providing affiliates with a commission on a sale of any product they promote. It is the easiest and the cheapest way of starting an online business as there is no need to go to the expense of creating and selling your own product. All you really need is a way of making a connection between your customers and the products you are promoting; if a sale is made through your link, you get the commission.

There are loads of affiliate networks so do spend some time analyzing each one and deciding if it fits your needs or not. Once you have signed up to a program, you will be given a tracking link, which you use to promote the products. One thing to be aware of with affiliate programs is that there are three different payment types so make sure you pick the one that suits you:

- **PPC** – Pay Per Click. You make your money based on how many people are referred to the website of the advertiser via your website. No purchase is necessary by the visitor but don't expect to get vast amounts of money this way; most PC programs pay very little and it takes a long time to build up a decent sum.

- **PPS** – Pay Per Sale. Your commission is paid when a sale is completing using your unique affiliate link and will be a set percentage of the sale price.

- **PPL** – Pay Per Lead. You get paid every time one of your visitors inputs their contact details on the advertiser's site.

How to Make Money

Learn How to Start An Online Business For FREE: www.lacobizonlinebusiness.com

As you probably guessed, affiliate marketing is passive income. It is also one of the most competitive forms of online business but is, provided you do your homework well, an easy way to earn money. To gain success, you need to understand what works and what clearly doesn't while you promote your chosen products.

Patience

There are loads of affiliate marketing websites so patience is key here. Make sure you add high-quality relevant content to your website regularly so you move higher in the Google search rankings; the higher you are, the more likely people are to visit your site. You can also join relevant forums and discussions to meet potential new customers. At this stage, it is all about developing your brand and awareness of it.

Choose Your Products Carefully

The biggest mistake you can make is to join several affiliate programs and promote everything you can think of. You want to be able to give them all enough attention and you won't get the results you want. Start with one affiliate site and choose products that are attractive and can reach a large market. To do that, you need to understand the requirements of your audience and pick your products to suit.

More Sources of Traffic

The way you make your money is through traffic to your website and the more you can get to go to your sales page, the better. Try using Google AdWords to make your own sales ad and using it to direct traffic to your sales site from different sources.

Targeted Traffic

Learn How to Start An Online Business For FREE: www.lacobizonlinebusiness.com

The only way you are going to make money is to push visitors to your site but first you have to attract those visitors. You can do this in four different ways – free ads, paid ads, email marketing or article marketing. With paid advertising you need a combination of an ad, decent graphics and a link whereas with free ads, you can place a link on any free advertising site, such as Craigslist.

For the email marketing you embed an option on your website for people to sign up to your email list. Article marketing is a little more difficult – for anyone to believe in you, you need to be quite high in the search engine rankings first; then you can start writing articles and linking to your affiliate site. You can choose any of the article directories online such as Ezine Articles; simply submit your article to your chosen directory and other affiliates will republish it. As your article gets republished it, you creep up the search engine ranks.

Testing, Measuring, Tracking

Every action must be tested and the performance measured so that you can see what is and isn't working. The tracking results will tell you whether you should keep, change or boot an action. For example, if your banner ads don't seem to be gaining you a great deal, try putting them in different places around your website. Monitor the results and compare them because some areas will definitely earn you more money than others.

Research Demand

This goes hand in hand with understanding the market requirements. If you are getting a good level of traffic to your website, have a look at your sales charts – daily, weekly, etc., to see what customers are looking at and buying. If you don't have

Learn How to Start An Online Business For FREE:
www.lacobizonlinebusiness.com

this information, which you won't have as a new business, spend the time researching the product and how it meets the demands of the user.

Always Research and Follow New Methods/Techniques

Trends in digital marketing are dynamic to say the least and so is affiliate marketing. Always keep yourself updated with all the newest methods and techniques if you want to be successful. If your results are out of date, you will fall far behind your competitors; keep up with the latest trends, and you will be in the running.

Use the Right Advertiser

If your visitors purchase a product that you promote and they are not happy with it, they won't come back. It may not be your fault; it could be the fault of the advertiser but your credibility is what suffers. Make sure you choose high-quality advertisers that offer great customer service and your reputation will be intact.

Make Use of Tools

Make use of tools that can help your campaign to be more effective and efficient. There are loads of tools that help you to do research on the market, research on your competitors, track your ad campaigns and convert them. You can also use tools that test out your affiliate links for you and let you know if any are broken so you can fix them.

Affiliate marketing is one of the best ways of making a passive income. Although you can't sit back and watch the money roll in without lifting a finger, get it right and you won't have too much work to do once you are set up. All you need is a website, some great content on a regular basis, a way of attracting visitors and

Learn How to Start An Online Business For FREE:
www.lacobizonlinebusiness.com

a couple of great affiliate programs. Do be prepared for hard work at the start though; without it your efforts will fail spectacularly!

Top 15 Affiliate Networks

Let's take a look at some of the best affiliate networks out there. Have a look at the information, take a look at their websites and draw your own conclusions as to which ones meet your needs. Narrow your search down and start with just one:

ShareASale

ShareASale is one of the long-term affiliate sights, and has been operating for more than 15 years now. And they are one of the few networks that have made sure to keep up with the times. Their marketplace is packed with products from merchants that cater to just about every need or whim you could think of, making them one of the top affiliate networks ever.

Pros

- They offer flexibility in payouts with both standard and digital options. Not many networks offer digital payouts so this is a big plus.

- They have a huge selection of products, one of the widest available on any affiliate network, which means there will always be something to promote regardless of your chosen niche.

Cons

They aren't quite as straightforward as some of the other networks and it will take more time for you to get set up. This

Learn How to Start An Online Business For FREE:
www.lacobizonlinebusiness.com

isn't a huge problem but you will need to have some technical knowledge.

Amazon Associates

Amazon is a household name, the largest online marketplace in the world and it is packed with millions of products that can be delivered in one day. There is something for every niche here, making it one of the best starting points for any affiliate marketer.

Pros

- You can earn up to 10% on some product sales via your affiliate link

- Any purchase made by any traffic referred from you earns you commission, whether it is the product you promoted or not. So, if a visitor clicks on your link but buys a different product, you still get the revenue.

- The most diverse range of products found anywhere, the largest one-stop-shop that tends to result in larger orders than the single product link a visitor clicks on.

Cons

- The cookie in your affiliate link expires after 24 hours so any purchases made outside of that time will not get you any revenue.

- There are few options for payout – bank transfer, check or Amazon Gift Card. It is hoped that they will add a digital payment option in the near future.

eBay Partners

Learn How to Start An Online Business For FREE: www.lacobizonlinebusiness.com

Even eBay is offering an affiliate program; it's as simple as finding the products that you want to promote and using the tools offered by the eBay Partner Network to help you.

Pros

- The most diverse marketplace in the world, eBay is user-based and you can find anything that you want.

- It is incredibly straightforward to use; there are no complicated rules, all you need to do is share your link for the products you choose and, if someone buys it, you earn the money.

- For the first three months, you get double the commission, a great way to kickstart your earnings potential.

Cons

- If an auction you are promoting doesn't end within 10 days you won't get any revenue, regardless of whether the winning bidder came via you or not.

Neutral

- Instead of, as it is with other programs, it being you and the affiliate eBay is also factored into the equation which means every sale is split into three. Your commission is based on the portion that eBay gets, not the affiliate product owner. It can work but you must be aware of how it works.

Shopify Affiliate Program

Learn How to Start An Online Business For FREE: www.lacobizonlinebusiness.com

Shopify is one of the largest providers of eCommerce software in the world and most people have heard of it. If you choose a niche where your audience is also attempting to sell on the Internet, Shopify is the best partnership for you to direct them to. Basically, you are referring online sellers to Shopify as a platform for them to set up an online store.

Pros

- You can earn quite a lot with each referral. It is perfectly possible to earn a bounty of 200%, your first couple of months' fee for a referral subscription. This can equate to up to $598 on a standard plan. The bounty on the enterprise plan is 100%, equal to $2000.

- It is one of the best platforms to refer others too as it the leading e-commerce contender.

Cons

- The payout may be great but the audience you refer must be online sellers otherwise Shopify will never be anywhere near relevant to them.

Clickbank

Clickbank is similar to ShareASale and is another wide-ranging marketplace full of merchants that you can choose to promote, based on your niche.

Pros

- You have a fantastic range of products to choose from and their database is one of the easiest to work through, making your job easy.

Learn How to Start An Online Business For FREE: www.lacobizonlinebusiness.com

Cons

- Unlike ShareASale, they don't offer any form of digital payout. They offer direct bank deposit, check, wire transfer or Payoneer.

- You can't earn any more than $150 for each referral sale, irrespective of what the product is. That is somewhat limiting and can put people off.

Rakuten Marketing Affiliates

Rakuten is one of the top online stores and it offers pretty much anything; they cater to all niches and are happy to pay you to help them sell.

Pros

- Rakuten is a trusted name, a store that has won awards and has partnerships with huge brands, including the NBA, meaning you can promote their products with complete confidence.

Cons

- It takes time to set up because each individual brand that you choose to promote must be set up individually. However, it does make you think hard about the brands you are promoting

- It isn't very easy to get around their knowledge base and their help articles are not very straightforward. They do have a good support team on hand though.

Leadpages Partner Program

Learn How to Start An Online Business For FREE: www.lacobizonlinebusiness.com

Leadpages is one of the most powerful marketing tools online. Every individual, regardless of expertise can easily create a top-selling landing page and their product is pretty much unrivaled. If your audience is a digital one, looking to set up great landing pages, this is the program for you.

Pros

- Provided your audience is the right one, this one will sell itself. Leadpages have made their product so good, all you need to do is show it to those who already have web pages and sales are pretty much guaranteed.

- It is powerful and that makes it worth the effort to promote it.

- Their payouts are huge, offering an impressive 30% on every sale and that commission continues for as long as the customer continues to spend.

Cons

- It is limited to a specific niche and will sell really well but only to that specific audience. It is not something you can promote on any affiliate website so you must be certain of your audience.

StudioPress Affiliate

StudioPress is, like Leadpages, also limited in niche but it is worth going after if your audience is the right one. StudioPress creates WordPress Hosting and WordPress themes are responsive, customizable and adaptable.

Pros

Learn How to Start An Online Business For FREE: www.lacobizonlinebusiness.com

- This is another of those products that will sell itself because most WordPress users will take one look at it and fall for it, making your job incredibly easy.

- Their payouts are very generous; they pay 35% commission on theme sales and a $75 minimum sale per site.

Cons

- It is limited to audiences that want an online presence established and regardless of niche, that is a growing demand but it still won't suit all users.

CJ Affiliate Publishers

CJ Affiliate has been involved in affiliate marketing for 20 years and their expertise shows in everything that they do. They offer products to suit all niches, making it easy for you to find something to promote.

Pros

- They are one of the biggest affiliate networks in the world, pretty much unrivaled in size.

- They are a network that you can easily rely on; while they are not infallible, 20 years and going strong in business shows that they adapt to dynamic shifts in requirements and move with the times.

Cons

- Their application process is in-depth and you can expect to be scrutinized very closely before they will accept you.

Learn How to Start An Online Business For FREE: www.lacobizonlinebusiness.com

They want high standards and that is one of the factors in their success.

Bluehost Affiliate Program

Bluehost is one of the top hosts for WordPress users. Their process is affordable, their packages are flexible and their customer support is second to none. All you do is refer people to them.

Pros

- The referral process is straightforward. All you do is sign up for free, put your referral link on your website and get paid a commission for any sale made on any Bluehost package through that link.

- They are recommended by WordPress as the best host for the platform and you won't get a better recommendation than that.

Cons

- Once again the audience for this is limited to those who are looking for a web host. You can advertise it all you like; if it isn't what your audience wants, you won't make any money from it.

- The payout minimum for the first year after your first referral is $100. That may not seem too difficult to meet but it is an unnecessary payout deadline.

ConvertKit Affiliate Program

ConvertKit is one of the top platforms for email marketing. It is fully customizable to user requirements and fits each individual
Learn How to Start An Online Business For FREE: www.lacobizonlinebusiness.com

user uniquely. They are a recommended name within the industry.

Pros

- If your audience is looking for an email marketing platform they won't get better than this as it serves every need a user could possibly want.

- Provided referred users continue to have an active account, you continue to get paid. There are no cut-off points.

Cons

- Email marketing isn't used by everybody so this won't suit all audiences – it may not be the affiliate you need.

- Because ConvertKit offers users a 30-day money-back guarantee, no questions asked, each time a referral signs up, you have to wait a minimum of 30 days for your commission to be confirmed.

MaxBounty Affiliate Network

MaxBounty is one of the newer affiliate networks but it is already showing promise by working with some huge brand names, including T-Mobile, McAffee and Norton. They take great pride in the fact that they do things other networks don't do and, so far it's working for them.

Pros

- If you earn at least $1000 per month for the first three months after you sign up, they will give a bonus of $1000.

Learn How to Start An Online Business For FREE:
www.lacobizonlinebusiness.com

- Where many programs are fixed on monthly payouts, MaxBounty offers weekly payouts.

- They offer digital options for payouts, something else that many networks don't offer – a big plus for them

- They offer a reward system for the affiliate earners that top the list, making it more competitive and fun to use than many other networks.

Cons

- They aren't established as much as other platforms; in a few years they may be one of the best but, right now, it's too early to tell.

Google AdSense

Google AdSense is another well-known name but, rather than being an affiliate platform they are an online advertiser instead. However, if you have a blog, it is one of the best-known ways to earn money and the affiliate principles are the same – you promote something and get paid when your audience shows interest in it.

Pros

- There isn't any need to look for products to promote. Google AdSense provides the adverts, all you have to do is make sure there is a space on your website.

- You have control of what type of adverts are shown and can disable any that don't match your site.

Learn How to Start An Online Business For FREE:
www.lacobizonlinebusiness.com

- There is no doubting that this is one of the most reputable of all online platforms. Everyone knows Google, no need for you to build up any credibility.

Cons

- You need to be able to determine that one or more of the ads is a problem before you can take steps to address it. You won't see any of the ads so you need your audience to tell you if there is a problem.

Tapgerine

Tapgerine is an advertising program that is targeted at mobile users. They may be a little more limited in what they offer but for the mobile marketers they do quite well.

Pros

- They are not trying to conquer all, instead focusing on something quite specific and doing it well.

Cons

- Their payment structure isn't very easy to fathom and their knowledge base is quite limited. However, they are quite new and this should all change as they grow.

- They are still small and to be fair, mobile advertising isn't very niche. This means that they don't really stand out even though they specialize in the mobile marketing area.

Chikita Publishers Network

Learn How to Start An Online Business For FREE: www.lacobizonlinebusiness.com

Another website for online advertising, much like AdSense and with just as good a reputation. They make this list if for nothing else other than sheer popularity.

Pros

- They are a trustworthy platform with a solid reputation built up over years of providing top quality advertising and content- no spam here.

Cons

- They may be a respected and knowledgeable business with a fantastic amount of support but they are not Google, and recommending them over Google is not very easy to do.

This should have given you an idea of what affiliate programs are all about and some that you can work with straightaway. The most important thing that will decide your choice is your audience and their needs. Go ahead, pick a couple, do some research and get started with earning money on affiliate marketing.

Learn How to Start An Online Business For FREE: www.lacobizonlinebusiness.com

Blogging

Blogging is an incredibly popular way of making money online and there are three steps to follow:

1. Setup your blog and get started on establishing yourself as a top authority in your chosen niche. You do this by creating and publishing relevant high-quality content on a regular basis.

2. Choose your streams of income and implement them – make sure they are relevant to your niche

3. Keep interacting online with other people to keep your blog at the front of their thoughts

Your ultimate goal is to ensure that your blog becomes THE source of information about your topic and, as visitors arrive, you can make money through any of your chosen income streams.

So, how does this work?

Successful bloggers ensure that their blog is a home base where their income streams are run from. It is important to have one central place to get your message across, a place where you will always be. Some of the income streams you can add to a blog include:

- Affiliate marketing
- Advertising
- Selling your own products – physical or digital
- Selling your own services

Learn How to Start An Online Business For FREE:
www.lacobizonlinebusiness.com

While having one stream of income may not make you much having several can add up and the beauty of blogging is that, provided they are relevant you can have several streams going at the same time.

How Much?

How much you can make will depend on many factors; some make an absolute mint, others bring in a reasonable income while some barely make any money at all. The possibilities for earning income are endless but there is no guaranteed amount that you will earn. It isn't the easiest way either but the only limit is you. The more creative you are, the more you stand to earn.

It isn't very easy to find any solid figures about blogging income either but although many have stopped doing it, some bloggers will still publish an income report. When you read these, there are two things you need to be aware of:

- **There is a difference between net income and total revenue.** Many of these income reports will have the total revenue figures on them and it's hard to find the actual net income or the profit. You might read an income report that claims a fantastic income figure but, most of the time this will be total revenue. Read a bit further and you might find that half that revenue amount or more is spent on advertising, not to mention the rest of the expenses, like hosting, etc. on top of that. Actual profit is very low. Of course you may come across these that make a huge amount of money without the massive expenditure but these are rare.

Learn How to Start An Online Business For FREE: www.lacobizonlinebusiness.com

- **Every blogger has their own unique circumstances so drawing a general conclusion is not easy.** You might come across a blogger who makes good money on the topic that you intend to write about. This doesn't mean that you will be able to get the same results. There are far too many variables involved and far too many combinations of income streams and your results may be wildly different.

How Long?

Making money through blogging is not easy nor is it a five-minute job. It can take many hours every week to build your blog and maintain it to the highest of quality and most bloggers work for at least a month before they see any money from their hard work.

In reality, you should allow up to six months before you make any kind of decent income and that will only be a part-time income. For a consistently good income, expect one or two years of hard work. Obviously there will always be exceptions to the rule but not many.

It certainly is not realistic to expect to start a blog now and be earning big money within a couple of months. There is a lot of learning to be done first, and much time to be spent on building your website your content, social media pages, not to mention, relationships with followers and your own credibility.

If you are looking to make a quick buck, blogging isn't for you but don't be put off. If you want to start slow, blogging is a good option. It's something you can do as a part-time job and is well worth putting in the effort.

Learn How to Start An Online Business For FREE:
www.lacobizonlinebusiness.com

How?

There are five main streams of income that bloggers use to make money:

Advertising

Every company wants their product or service under the noses of potential customers and that means they might want to place an advert on your blog provided your audience is their audience. Here's how adverts can be incorporated on a blog:

- **Display** – graphics that go in your content, your website header or footer or in the sidebar

- **Reviews and Giveaways** – a company may give you a free product, some will also provide financial compensation as well, so long as you promote that specific item on your blog usually by way of a product review.

- **Underwritten or Sponsored posts** – you can get paid by money to write a post that mentions them and/or their products.

- **Newsletters/Podcasts/Video Sponsorship** – adverts are placed into your emails or as small ad breaks in a podcast or video.

This is one of the easiest forms of earning income and that makes it a popular method for bloggers. However, it doesn't bring in the money that it used to in the early days, mainly because so many people are doing it, and to bring in any real profit, you need a lot of traffic. Also, you could end up royally peeing off your visitors if you have too many ads- you've been on

Learn How to Start An Online Business For FREE: www.lacobizonlinebusiness.com

those websites before, where you can't see the content for the ads! It is worth doing though, just to bring in a few extra pennies.

Affiliate Marketing

As you learned earlier, with affiliate marketing, you promote the products for another company and link to the products. When your visitors click your link and make a purchase you earn a commission. It isn't always dependent on a purchase; sometimes, all the visitor has to do is fill in their details or sign up for a service. There are thousands to make your choice from and we mentioned 15 of them earlier.

Affiliate marketing can be one of the most lucrative of all income streams. You can promote products that you love without having to create the product and maintain it. Provided you keep your blog up to date with relevant content, this should be a relatively easy way to make some money. Again, don't expect it to happen overnight.

Digital Products

Digital products are an easy way to make some money and many bloggers create their own and sell them. You don't need to hold any inventory and you can easily and quickly distribute them with little to no risk and overhead. Some ideas include:

- **Online Courses** – create a course based around something you know and sell it as many times as you want
- **Online Workshops or Courses** – The same as above but live.

Learn How to Start An Online Business For FREE: www.lacobizonlinebusiness.com

- **eBooks** – write about a subject you know and self-publish it, selling one book over and again

- **Premium Content -** people must pay a fee to access this type of content on your website

- **Membership** – offer a membership for a set monthly or yearly fee, giving them access to content and features not available otherwise

- **Photos** – try selling your photos online

- **Audio/Video** – create voice-overs, music jingles, video clips and so on

- **Apps, Themes, Plugins** – if you are clever at coding these are great ways to make money

This is another good stream of income and brings you in a tidy sum on a regular basis.

- **Physical Products**

- Physical products are another big blogging seller, including:

- **Books** – some bloggers go on to publish traditional books based on their blogging

- **Handmade** – can you make something to sell?

- **Manufactured** – got a product that you can get a manufacturer to make for you?

- **Retail Arbitrage** – find great deals and sell them at a decent profit on Amazon and other similar sites.

Learn How to Start An Online Business For FREE:
www.lacobizonlinebusiness.com

- **Conferences, Events or Classes in-Person** – you provide something that others will buy a ticket to watch or listen to.

Physical products have become very popular in recent times but, while you can turn a profit, if you need to involve manufacturers, store inventory, handling, shipping and so on, things can get quite complicated. You can use drop shipping to get around some of this and we'll be looking in detail at that later on.

- **Services**

- If you have some kind of expertise that you relate your blog to, you can sell that expertise for money, either virtually or locally. Examples include:

- **Speaking** – some bloggers have turned to speaking gigs resulting from their niche and blog

- **Freelancing** – offer your expertise on a freelance basis, for example, graphic design, writing, etc.

- **Organization, Cookery, Decorating, Etc.** – some bloggers will offer a physical service to local subscribers or readers

This is a great way of making money quite quickly because you have little to no startup costs, your inventory is low and you get money for a skill or expertise you already possess. There is just one downside – you cannot scale this because your time is at a premium and you can only earn what your time allows.

Starting a Blog

Learn How to Start An Online Business For FREE:
www.lacobizonlinebusiness.com

Starting a blog is really quite simple and once you have done it, you should concentrate your efforts on building up a backlog of quality blog posts, at least 10 to 20. They must be relevant, high quality, full of information and current. Keep in mind that you want to be THE source for your niche.

The next thing to do is work out what your income streams are going to be and add them in one at a time until something stands out as working for you. While you are doing that, work on building up your social media relationships, in drawing in your potential audience. Don't get stuck on only promoting your stuff; get involved in conversations, and make sure you always respond to comments directed at you. Eventually, people will start looking to you for information.

Can you start a blog for free and make some money? Yes you can but it isn't a good idea and there is a good reason for that. When free services are used, that has more control over your website than you do and this is quite a risk, especially if you are intending to rely on the money you make. The best way to start is to use a self-hosted WordPress blog and shortly I will be walking you through how to do this.

First, a few tips on how to make that all-important income:

- Don't stop at one stream if income; use as many as you can manage easily. The key here is diversification.

- Long-term success can only come through hard work and on a blog, the key is strong, regular, reliable content. Don't bother trying to find a way around this because there isn't one.

Learn How to Start An Online Business For FREE:
www.lacobizonlinebusiness.com

- Every blogger chooses different ways to make money. There's no right way to do it and that is what makes this such a nice way of making money. The possibilities are endless, all you need to do is find what works best for you.

- Don't copy other bloggers, you won't win their audience from them that way. Instead, look for another way, something unique that fills a gap in the market.

The most successful bloggers didn't start out blogging for money; they started because they had a topic they were genuinely passionate about and wanted to share with others, a topic they can happily continue to write about for as long as they want to. The money comes as a great sideline for them.

Creating Your Blog

Before we begin, understand that there are two WordPress websites and both are different. WordPress.com is a commercial website that offers a complete solution for building and hosting a website whereas WordPress.org is the self-hosted version where you need to purchase hosting and a domain name separately. Don't be fooled into thinking that the all-in-one is the best option; with the self-hosted version you have far more control. With that said, let's get into using WorkPress.org to build our blog.

Hosting and Domain

Before you can even begin to think about building your blog, you need two things if you are to make your blog so that everyone can see it – a domain name and a hosting plan:

Learn How to Start An Online Business For FREE:
www.lacobizonlinebusiness.com

- The domain name is the address of your blog, the name of your company if you like. We talked about coming up with a name earlier so you should already have some good ideas in mind.

- The hosting plan is how people will see your site, the engine that gives it power. Every website and blog on the Internet is powered by a hosting plan of some sort.

- Both of these can be purchased from the same company so long as it is a reputable one. Run a search on the Internet for WordPress hosts and pick the one that suits you. Two that offer great service are SiteGround and BlueHost:

- Both are affordable and cost just a few dollars per month to host your blog

- WordPress is installed with a single click from the host; you do not need any technical knowledge.

- Both are reliable and fast to load. For what you pay, you get an excellent service in both reliability and speed, two very important factors in hosting a successful blog.

- Choose your host and pick the hosting plan you want – be very sure it offers exactly what you want and make sure you read the small print. Input the domain name that you want to use and then enter your personal and billing details. Each hosting plan will differ in setup so follow the instructions with yours carefully. Add any additional services you need but be careful here – when you start up you probably won't need these services; they just increase

Learn How to Start An Online Business For FREE:
www.lacobizonlinebusiness.com

your bill. Start basic and add services as and when you really need them.

- Make your purchase and complete the setup.

Installing WordPress

- If your chosen host includes one-click installation for WordPress, this is very easy. Simply open the welcome email you got from your host and login to your customer area. You should see a window that welcomes you to the first setup wizard. Make sure that the box for installing WordPress is ticked and continue with the setup.

- Next, input your login details – these are what you are going to use to login into your blog on WordPress so make them memorable for you. Now you can choose a theme for the blog. Please don't spend any real time on this step; pick a free one and later I will show you how to change it. When you see the Success screen, your WordPress blog is set up. To gain access to your dashboard, go to yourdomain.com/wp-admin. Input your own domain name and whatever ending you chose - .com, .co.uk, .org, etc.

Write a Post

Now you have a WordPress blog set up, you can write your very first post. This is extremely simple to do. In your dashboard area hover your mouse over the word Posts and then click on Add New. The editor will load and the steps are simple:

- Input a title for the post at the tops
- In the main box, type in your post content

Learn How to Start An Online Business For FREE: www.lacobizonlinebusiness.com

- Use the toolbar to format your post

- Click on Add Media to insert images

- On the right sidebar you can choose a category for your post

- Click on Publish to make the post public on your blog

Do take some time out to explore WordPress and all that it offers to get the best out of it.

Change the Way Your Blog Looks

One of the biggest benefits of using WordPress is the huge number of themes and plugins that you can access. A theme will help you to change the way your blog appears while a plugin adds additional functionality. Later, I will tell you some of the very best plugins to use but first, we'll look at themes.

The second your WordPress blog is created, it already has an active theme. This will be the theme you picked or, if you didn't, it will be the default theme. There are thousands more to choose from, many of them free so don't think you are limited to one or two.

Choosing a theme means choosing a free one or a premium one. The main difference between them is that the premium themes have more features and more details. For now stick with a free one, there's time enough to change to a paid one when business is booming.

To find a free one, either search the WordPress.org theme directory or have a look through a website called Just Free Themes.

Learn How to Start An Online Business For FREE:
www.lacobizonlinebusiness.com

For premium themes you will need a slightly different approach; run a search on Google for premium WP themes and see what comes up. You will also find premium themes in the WordPress theme directory.

Installing your chosen theme is easy:

- In your dashboard, go to Appearance and click on Themes

- Click on Add New

- For free themes from the official directory, search for a theme using its name and click on Install

- If you bought a premium theme, click on Upload Theme and install the file you would have received when you paid.

- Click Activate and the theme will go live on your blog.

Further Customizations

You can also use the WordPress Customizer to make other customizations to your site, allowing you to tweak things without having to do any coding. Click on Appearance and then on Customize.

Depending on which theme you have chosen, you may see different options on the left sidebar but generally you will be able to:

Use the left sidebar options to make changes

Preview them in real time using the button on the right

Learn How to Start An Online Business For FREE:
www.lacobizonlinebusiness.com

Save your changes and publish them to make them live on your blog.

Using Plugins

Themes dictate how your blog looks but plugins help to make it more functional. When you create a blog, all you can do is write and publish posts and create blog pages. With plugins you can add loads more, including:

- Social media buttons
- Contact forms
- Better SEO
- Backups

And so much more. Pretty much, if you can think of something you want on your blog, there will be a plugin for it. With more than 50,000 free ones and thousands more premium ones, you will find what you are looking for. For free ones, check the official plugin directory for WordPress and for premium ones, think of what functionality you want and then run a Google search for a plugin that will do the job. Do purchase only from reputable developers. You may find free plugins that offer a premium version too; these will be from reputable developers if you go through the official directory.

Best Plugins

There are loads of plugins that will only suit certain uses but there is also a load of plugins that every blog should use, including:

- UpdraftPlus – a backup plugin

Learn How to Start An Online Business For FREE: www.lacobizonlinebusiness.com

- Google Analytics
- Yoast SEO
- WP Super Cache
- Jetpack
- WPForms
- Wordfence Security

Installing a plugin is simple.

- In your dashboard click on Plugins and then on Add New
- For a free one, search using the name and click on Install Now
- For a premium one, click on Upload Plugin and install the file you were sent when you purchased it.
- Click on Activate and your plugins will be live

What Next?

When your blog is created and is looking and acting how you want it, what do you do next? Pretty much what you want but you will want to focus attention on advertising your blog to bring more traffic in and in setting up your income streams. Be prepared to put in the hours here; if you do not draw traffic in, your efforts are wasted so forget about making money for now and concentrate on making your blog and you visible and credible.

Learn How to Start An Online Business For FREE:
www.lacobizonlinebusiness.com

Facebook

Facebook is no longer anything new or exciting but there is no denying that it is the most popular of all the social media websites. With over 2 billion users active on a monthly basis, each day sees more than 1.3 billion users and those figures really can't be ignored, especially when you are looking for ways to get an income stream from your online business. It makes perfect sense to target such a huge and diverse audience.

However, it isn't easy and you will face many challenges along the way. For a start, the fact that is so large makes it hard to stand out from all the others. And now, because Facebook only displays certain posts on user timelines, the challenge is harder. It makes no difference how hard you work to create content and statuses for your Facebook page, the fact is only 2% of your audience will ever see them. This is down to the Facebook algorithm; whenever a user opens their feed the algorithm will go through a series of four steps in determining the posts they think the person should see:

- **Inventory** – the algorithm looks at the statuses shared by the user's friends and it will look at the pages they are following

- **Signals** – next, it will examine several signals taken from past behavior, including the person making the post, how much time was spent on the content, engagement with the content, tags, comments, whether the content is informative or not, and so on. One of the biggest signals for the moneymaking aspect is that the Facebook algorithm gives statuses a weighting, based on people considered to have more importance than the content on a page.

Learn How to Start An Online Business For FREE:
www.lacobizonlinebusiness.com

- **Prediction** – the signal will try to determine the reaction a story will get – will it be shared, will people comment on it, will they read it or will they just pass it by?

- **Score** – a Relevance Score is generated by the algorithm for each of the posts and that score is based on the previous steps.

When a user's feed is built up, the only posts shown will be those with the high relevance scores.

Business, Influencer or Just Ordinary?

We all know that the primary focus of Facebook is on being a social network. It's a place where users can get together, get social, and share things and chat. This is an important reason why the platform gives personal posts ore weighting than business page posts and this is something you are always going to have to keep in your mind – personal users will find it much easier to spread their word then a company will.

But nothing is ever as clear cut as it first seems.

Let's say that a person has just a small handful of friends on Facebook; they won't get their word out too far unless they have a way of producing content that is so fantastic that their friends share it among their own friends, and it continues to get shared, far and wide.

Alternatively, we could have a person who can get a lot of people to follow them, can interact regularly with them and they will find that their posts appear in more feeds than the person who doesn't have many friends.

Learn How to Start An Online Business For FREE: www.lacobizonlinebusiness.com

What you can take away from this is that, if you want people hearing what you have to say, you need to put the work in to get those people to support you and you need enough support to be considered an influencer. Once you get to that point, making money using Facebook is not difficult.

That said, do not push the thought of a business page to one side and ignore it. Provided your page is run properly, and provided you share relevant, high-quality content regularly, Facebook will take note and relevance scores will be increased accordingly.

Building Up Your Audience

If there is one reason why an influencer is highly successful on Facebook, it is that they have spent the time and effort on building up their audience first. How do they do this? The same way that you are going to do it, by sharing some top-quality content on a regular basis. It can be updated, on your blog posts, images, even links, so long as they are worthwhile and relevant. You need to build an area that you can excel in, something you have a real interest in and can show that you are an expert in that area.

Some businesses hire influencers to do their marketing for them but they also need to build up their presence on Facebook at the same time. Given time, they can use that presence to show people that they are, indeed, experts in their chosen niche. Take Starbucks for example they've done this so well that their business page now has more than 37 million people following it.

So, your Facebook fan page should have one primary goal – to be somewhere where followers can get to know who you are. If your content excites them, in time they will respect you and that is followed by trust. Ultimately, these people will likely be more

Learn How to Start An Online Business For FREE:
www.lacobizonlinebusiness.com

than happy to make a purchase from you and come back for more. There is one thing you should live by – instead of seeing your Facebook fans as nothing more than a commodity, you should see them as your friends.

Making Money from Facebook

So, onto making money. There are a few ways you can do this on Facebook and we'll discuss each one now:

Selling Products

You can do this on a specific Buy and Sell Group or in the Facebook Marketplace. The Marketplace is used a lot on Facebook and, depending on where you are located, you may see quite a lot of services and goods put up for sale. These will always be listed in categories, depending on what they are.

Facebook users can choose the area, geographically speaking, that they want to see For Sale ads from and can also filter by distance and by price. So, if you have physical products to sell, you could list them on the Marketplace. However, be aware that people like to haggle and negotiate price so keep in mind what the lowest price you will sell at is.

There are also lots of Buy and Sell groups you can choose. Pick one that suits your region and audience and post your goods for sale there. Because these tend to have a more settled audience, there is less negotiation for the price.

Another place you can try to sell from is your own business page but this isn't quite so easy. Relevance scores don't tend to be high enough and your posts are unlikely to appear in newsfeeds. So it comes back to posting regular high-quality content. If there

Learn How to Start An Online Business For FREE:
www.lacobizonlinebusiness.com

is one formula you should apply it is this – Being useful + Being authentic + selling occasionally = good Sales on Facebook.

If you choose to go down the route of influencer marketing you can use your influencers to help you; they will post the content and they will send their followers to you.

Facebook advertising is also a way of getting your posts to go further but, it is important to realize that, if you want to build a genuine audience, only a small number of your posts can be sales-oriented. The rest have to be genuine valuable and provide information and some entertainment.

As far as Facebook Ads are concerned you must keep in mind that most users are found inside the Buying Cycle. They do not use Facebook with the ultimate aim of making a purchase; unlike Google where people search for items to buy, Facebook is used for socializing, catching up with old friends, work colleagues and watching videos – they don't come there to buy your products.

It is down to you to build up a sales funnel and the only way to do this is to reach out to as wide an audience as you can – that means sharing diverse content. You should provide readers with links to high-quality posts, to anecdotes or videos, statements, an infographic in short anything that could attract followers. These followers must relate in some way to the product you promote or they should be the type of people who are likely to buy your product.

Once you have your support base, start promoting by posting content. Be aware of what the level of engagement is on each post and, where engagement is high, share more of the same kind of content. Next, think about content promotion in ads that

Learn How to Start An Online Business For FREE:
www.lacobizonlinebusiness.com

get targeted at lookalike audiences. The chances are, these people will not have heard of you but their previous activities show that they are similar to the people who follow you. That means it should be quite easy to attract them to follow you.

Open a Group in Your Specific Niche

There isn't a great deal of value to be had in running groups on Facebook just to sell stuff but they are a great way of letting people know what your products or services are. They are very useful when you are selling products of an information type because a group can be set up and you can encourage your users to share their ideas and help one another. Again, it is important that your group be supplied with useful content and, every once in a while you can drop in a suggestion that your product will solve their problems.

Facebook Groups are best used as offshoots. Let's say that you offer an eBook or an online course for sale; a group could help people who purchase it to come together and discuss it, to provide their own insights or even ask for help.

Sales Funnels

To earn decent money on Facebook, there are seven steps to follow to build up your sales funnel. Do this gradually and build up to a sale, don't just jump straight in there.

Concentrate first on your 'warm' audience. These are the people who already show you they are interested in your product and you and you now need to keep them interested with quality content.

Next, find an audience of people who are interested in the same type of product or service and create a lookalike audience

Learn How to Start An Online Business For FREE:
www.lacobizonlinebusiness.com

Target that audience with a high-quality of content

Some of that audience will like it and will follow your page and some, if you are lucky, will even make a purchase

Using Facebook Pixels, target those who haven't made a purchase with a marketing email or reminder

Continue doing this to anyone who hasn't converted into a paying customer

Make sure your conversions are maximized.

Influencer Marketing

Some brands find it much harder to build their follower numbers up than others do and these are the ones that tend to look to influencers to help them.

The influencer has already done the hard work of building up a following; all influencers started off as nobody's on Facebook but they took the time and put in the effort necessary to get themselves established in their niche. They have taken the steps needed to build up trust and authority and that means they have a good following.

Influencers know that they can go into a partnership with a brand and can spread the message in a way that the brand could not do. The only real requirement is that the brand fits in with the people who follow the influencer. The influencer can do a couple of things, including sharing affiliate links and delivering content that is sponsored to their own followers.

On occasion, they can also be subtle in their promotion, even funny at times. Take The Meat Man in the UK. Hs business sells meat, both to the restaurants and to the public. He paid a
Learn How to Start An Online Business For FREE:
www.lacobizonlinebusiness.com

Facebook influencer from the UK to come up with a prank video where a man convinces his girlfriend that, instead of 5kg of chicken she ordered 00kg and gets a bill of ££2,000. Throughout the entire video, viewers can see the boxes of products clearly labeled with The Meat Man.

That one single Facebook influencer video pulled in over 7 million views in 2 days and resulted in The Meat Man receiving quite a bit of coverage in the press. To compare, his own Facebook page only has 10,000 likes and there was no way that he could have gotten that much publicity by himself.

For most serious businesses, the best option is to build a page on Facebook and work with a relevant influencer at the same time, just to get the process moving and get a reach that many brands can't achieve by themselves.

YouTube

YouTube videos litter the Internet; there's pretty much a video for everything these days and those that upload them, well, some of them are today's celebrities, self-made of course. These are people that have earned themselves a nice following because they upload video content that is aimed at teaching people, entertaining them, even video reviews and most of them do it just because they want to.

You are highly unlikely to start a YouTube channel just to make money but there are quite a few opportunities to do so once you start delving into it.

Subscribers

The one thing that you do need if you are to make money from YouTube is subscribers but how many do you need? Well,

Learn How to Start An Online Business For FREE:
www.1acobizonlinebusiness.com

according to New Media Rockstars, the top earners on YouTube pull in millions, some of them tens of millions but revenue will depend entirely on the channel and what it offers.

Have a look at the estimated earnings and the number of subscribers some of the top earners have:

- **EpicMealTime** – averages around $3.1 million with 7 million channel subscribers

- **Ray William Johnson** – averages at about $4.2 million with around 10 million channel subscribers

- **FunToyzCollector** – averages $30.4 million with around 8 million channel subscribers

This doesn't mean that the smear YouTube channels can't make money because the potential for earning doesn't depend only on how many views your videos get or how many subscribers you have. It is also dependent on how well you and your followers engage, what niche you chose, and how you choose to make your money. Before we start looking at how to make that al important income stream, you first need to understand your audience.

Your YouTube Audience

Building up an audience gives you what you need to monetize your YouTube channel in several different ways. However, to take full advantage of that, the first step is in understanding how your audience is made up.

The better the niche you are in, the deeper and more select you are, the more chance you have of getting together with good brands that want to target a particular audience. When you look

Learn How to Start An Online Business For FREE: www.lacobizonlinebusiness.com

at the demographics of your audience (by going to studio.youtube.com), pay attention to things like this:

- **Gender** - is your audience predominantly male, female or a fair mix of both?
- **Age** – does your audience fall into a specific age range or is it a broad range?

Geographic Location – are your audience from a particular location/city/country? Can you identify any brands that would suit specific locations?

With this knowledge at hand, you can understand your audience and you can get to work with brands.

Now you know how you are going to understand your audience, when you get one, we can look at how you will make money.

Making Money on YouTube

Just as they do with a blog or with Facebook, your audience has one of the keys to unlocking your potential for earning but the real key lies in how you create your revenue streams – not just one but several and there are a few you can choose from:

YouTube Partner and Ads

YouTube ads are most likely your first port of call but to use them you need to be a YouTube Partner. Open your YouTube account, go into the Channel menu, and verify your account and then you can enable Monetization.

Once you are a YouTube Partner, you will need Google AdSense. If you don't have an account head over to Google and create one.

Learn How to Start An Online Business For FREE:
www.lacobizonlinebusiness.com

You will need this if you are to make any money and get paid for your ads and to get your reports.

Now, in Video Manager, you should see a small green $ beside your videos. This will indicate whether a video has been monetized or not; click on that $ sign and you will see the specific monetization settings for that video.

It is easy enough to set up but believe me when I say that this isn't going to earn you a fortune – it's worth it for what you can make out of it though.

Beyond Adverts

In 2016, YouTube made a decision to be a lot more transparent about ads on their platform and people didn't take too kindly to it. Basically, they started using an algorithm to determine what videos were advertiser-friendly and what weren't and many YouTubers feared losing revenue from the ads that supported their channel, mainly because of the content.

YouTube says that content may be excluded from monetization by ads if they include any of the following:

- Content that is considered sexually suggestive, including humor of a sexual nature and partial nudity
- Violence, especially violent extremist acts and showing serious injury
- Language not considered appropriate, including vulgar language, harassment and profanity
- Anything that promotes the use, ale of and abuse of drugs and any other regulated substance

Learn How to Start An Online Business For FREE: www.lacobizonlinebusiness.com

- Events and subjects considered sensitive or controversial including those to do with war, natural disasters, political conflict, tragedy and so on, regardless of whether graphic images are used or not.

In reality, YouTube actually began the demonetization process in 2012; they just didn't want you to know. Videos would be demonetized without any warning and without the owner being told that it would happen, thus losing money immediately. Things have changed now because YouTube does tell video creators that it will happen and there is a process in place to contest a decision.

While advertising might be one of the most popular ways of making money from YouTube there is a large trade-off – YouTube retains about 45% of any revenue earned. Because of that, you really need to look at other streams of revenue so let's move on to the next one.

Selling Merchandise

This is actually quite a bit easier than you might think and many YouTubers sell physical products or services via their YouTube videos. And this brings you far more than just money in the bank.

It also widens the exposure that you get because your brand and your personality are out there, not just online but offline too. It works in favor of your relationships with your followers and your fans because not only are they seeing you online, they are buying into your brand too.

You can produce branded merchandise quite easily. Search online, you will find plenty of reputable places where you can

Learn How to Start An Online Business For FREE:
www.lacobizonlinebusiness.com

order designs for certain products. And for order handling, etc., you can integrate with Oberlo, or one of any of the other many Print-On-Demand companies that take care of order fulfillment, shipping and support. This is drop shipping at its finest but with less effort. We'll talk more about drop shipping later.

Another alternative is to go into partnership with a merchandising network that already exists for other creators. However, be aware that you will be in strong competition in an already crowded marketplace and you won't have so much control over when you add products, whether you can offer any discounts, how your content is integrated and all the rest that comes when you have an e-Commerce site of your own.

Once you have an audience, selling your merchandise gives you two great advantages:

- You get a content engine that is constantly working to drive traffic consistently to your e-Commerce store
- You get the trust of your audience, built on from serving them on a regular basis with free, quality content.

Both advantages that are designed to make any YouTube channel pretty jealous.

Crowdfunding

If the only thing standing between your great idea and making it a reality is money, then you should consider crowdfunding. Crowdfunding is a great way of raising cash to put a product into production, to hire actors, to buy equipment to make your videos better and so on. Provided you have a compelling enough idea, it's worth pitching it to your audience and the community that makes up crowdfunding.

Learn How to Start An Online Business For FREE: www.lacobizonlinebusiness.com

Many people that go for crowdfunding offer a preview of what their product or idea is so you should think about shooting a short video to explain it or to provide an idea of what's on offer. Some of the best crowdfund sites that go well with YouTube campaigns include:

- **Kickstarter** – one of the best-known, this one has a track record for being able to raise money for cool and creative ideas and projects. Do set a goal that can be attained because you only get the money if that goal is set.

- **Indiegogo** – an alternative with funding options that are somewhat more flexible

There are other crowdfunding sites but these are the most popular.

Fan Funding

Fan funding is like crowdfunding but it's your audience that provides your cash injection by way of donations. You, as a video creator, give your voice to the net for free; you don't charge your audience a penny to gain from your knowledge but you can set up a donation system. If your content is good enough, your readers may well opt to donate towards your cause.

Some of the most popular options for fan funding platforms include:

- **YouTube Fan Funding** – this is a YouTube feature that allows you to provide your audience with a sort of tips jar. They can donate what they want, when they want but you do, obviously need a YouTube account for this.

Learn How to Start An Online Business For FREE:
www.lacobizonlinebusiness.com

- **Patreon** – this is a membership platform that lets creators get paid for their work. Creator fans can subscribe to their favorites for a dollar a month and the rewards are quite exhaustive.

- **Tippee** – Provides a way of getting both recurring and one-off donations.

Again, there are others but these are the first you should look at.

Content Licensing

If one of your videos goes viral to millions of people, you can consider licensing that video in exchange for cash. If your video has enough appeal you could find that other content creators, news sites online, news outlets, morning shows and so on may even reach out to you to buy the right to use that video.

You could also consider listing licensed videos in a specific marketplace like Juken Media; this will make it much easier for people to find your video and buy the rights to it.

Working with Brands

More and more, brands are turning to influencer marketing, investing money in their own futures with marketers who have already built up and gained loyalty from their audience. This is a huge opportunity for any creator, including you provided you can get the right deal.

Establishing a baseline fee should be done by looking at how many views your videos get on average and then multiplying that figure by between $0.05 and $0.15 per view. This is typically what most brands will pay for views through ads on YouTube.

Learn How to Start An Online Business For FREE:
www.lacobizonlinebusiness.com

Depending on what leverage you have, be it demographics, quality of your content, profitability and uniqueness of your content, and so on, you may, provided the Brand is a great fit, be able to negotiate better.

When you enter into a partnership with content sponsored by a brand, you must be completely transparent. Never agree to endorse anything you do not believe in, or like, and always tell your audience what you are doing and why.

Some of the best influencer marketplaces where your channel can be added so you get discovered by the brands include:

- **Grapevine Logic** – a very popular marketplace for influencers; the only requirement for joining is that your channel has at least 1000 followers.

- **Famebit** – offers many brands and the opportunity to find a great sponsorship deal. Your channel must have 5000 followers before you can join.

- **Channel Pages** – allows you to partner with brands and with other YouTube creators

- **Crowdtap** – you do small tasks centered on content creation and get paid in cash or with other rewards. You can have as little as one follower to join.

You will find that some of the marketplaces offer free goods while others have the biggest brands that will pay the money. Find what suits you but get your channel listed wherever you can to make sure you are completely visible.

Another way of doing this is to become an affiliate marketer for relevant brands and make a passive income via sales

Learn How to Start An Online Business For FREE:
www.lacobizonlinebusiness.com

commissions, in the same way that you would affiliate marketing through your own blog. You could review the products using YouTube review videos on your own channel. There is no risk to the brand because they will only pay you when a sale comes in via your affiliate link and there's no risk to you because you do not lay out any money to be their affiliate marketer.

Choose larger affiliate programs like Clickbank, which pays up to 75% commission or the Amazon Affiliate Network, which pays up to 10 per sale. You could also look for other brands within your niche, ones that have their own programs, not uncommon these days.

Selling Without Being Annoying

So far, most of the strategies we discussed involve directly promoting your store, your products, service, whatever it is you are offering, or promoting a crowdfunding or fan-funding campaign. You want your audience to see all this but it must be done in such a way that they don't start to see you as anything more than an annoyance.

That said, if you don't promote your business then you won't get any sales so how do you do it?

Placement

There are several different places that your ads and promotions can go where they will garner the most attention but won't irritate your audience:

CTA

Learn How to Start An Online Business For FREE: www.lacobizonlinebusiness.com

You can use your YouTube videos to add a call to action (CTA). You often see it at the end of a video and in the blurb underneath it – "if you liked this video, hit like/subscribe/follow".

A lot of YouTube video creators use this method because it helps to grow their followers and promotes their products without being too in your face. If you suggest to your audience what you would like them to do, they are more likely to do it. And this approach can also be used to direct the audience to purchase your product.

YouTube Cards

A YouTube Card is a great way to grab the attention of your audience, provided they are already engaged in your video. Cards can be used to promote your own stuff or the brand that you are in partnership with and can be timed to appear in your video at just the right minute – so long as they are timed properly, are relevant and don't distract from your main message, they can have quite an impact.

Links

One easy way of sending viewers to your online store or to wherever you want to direct them is to add links into the descriptions below your videos.

Using Other Platforms

It doesn't really matter that you have chosen YouTube as your main platform for promotion, there are plenty of other platforms to take advantage of. Use social media, a blog, guest posts, any other way you can think of to put your promotion out there. The more locations your message can be found in, the

Learn How to Start An Online Business For FREE:
www.lacobizonlinebusiness.com

more chance you have of it being seen and that increases the chances of your YouTube following growing.

YouTubepreneurs Are On the Rise

Most YouTube Video creators do not even consider the money when they start out; it's just a way of sharing something they love with the world. But, interested or not, that is exactly what puts them in a fantastic position to make a ton of money in a world that is completely obsessed with digital content.

The hardest part will be holding onto your audience but with great video content that will come easier as you go on. Just remember – be creative in how you opt to monetize your YouTube channel and you can have a decent stream of income in good time.

Learn How to Start An Online Business For FREE: www.lacobizonlinebusiness.com

A Word on Order Types

When you look at orders for both buying and selling, you will see a number of different types. These are the terms you need to learn:

- **Ask** – this is for buyers and is the price that a seller is willing to sell their stock for

- **Bid** – this is for sellers and is the price that a buyer is willing to pay for the stock

- **Spread** – this indicates the difference between the lowest asking price and the highest bidding price

- **Market Order** – this is a request for the stock to be bought or sold very quickly but at the best price available

- **Limit Order** – this is a request for the stock to be bought or sold at a specified or better price

- **Stop Order** – sometimes called a stop-loss order; when a specified price is reached for a stock, known as the stop level or stop price, an order gets executed and the whole order gets fulfilled at that price

- **Stop-Limit Order** – when the stop is reached, a trade becomes a limit order and will be fulfilled to the point where price limits already specified may be successfully met

There are other order types that you will come across but these will be more complex; ignore those for now and stick with these. Keep one thing in mind; many investors with very successful

Learn How to Start An Online Business For FREE: www.lacobizonlinebusiness.com

investment careers have done it using just two of those order types – market and limit.

The Market Order

The market order is an indication that you are prepared to buy or sell at the best price available on the market at the time. With a market order there are no parameters on price for the trade and that means the orders are executed with immediate effect and are completely filled – the only exception to that would be if you were attempting to purchase a million or more shares and trying to carry out a company coup!

If the price you receive or pay for the stock is not the price that was quoted to you a few seconds before, don't be too surprised. The fluctuation in ask and bid prices are constantly fluctuating as the day goes on. For that reason, market orders are best used for the purchases of stocks whose prices do not swing widely – blue-chip stock (the large ones) rather than small companies that may be more volatile.

Things to Know:

- Market orders are best used by buy-hold investors because they are not overly bothered by small price differences; it is more important to them that the trade gets completely executed.

- If market orders are placed after trading hours, after the markets have closed down for the day, the order is placed at the start of business the following day at the prevailing price.

- Do make sure you read your broker's disclaimer about trade execution. Some of the lower-cost brokers will pull

Learn How to Start An Online Business For FREE: www.lacobizonlinebusiness.com

all of your trade requests together for execution at a prevailing price and this will be done either at the close of the business day or at another specified time or day.

Limit Orders

Limit orders provide you with far more control over the execution price of the trade. If a stock trades at $50 per share but you think that a price of $40 fits in better with your valuation for the company, a limit order would be used to inform your broker that they are to hold and only execute at the point the ask price reaches $40. From a seller's point of view, limit orders are used to inform the broker that the shares or stocks cannot be sold until they reach that specified level.

Limit orders are great tools for the investor who buys and sells the stocks for smaller companies, stocks that tend have bigger spreads, dependent entirely upon the activity of the investors. They are also ideal for the person who wants to invest when the market is undergoing a period of instability over the short-term or when price beats fulfillment in terms of the order.

Other conditions can be placed on limit orders so you get more control over the length of time the order stays open. AON, or All or None orders, are executed only when every share that you are trading becomes available at the price limit you specify. GFD, or Good for Day orders, expire when the trading day is finished whether an order has been completely filled. And GTC, or Good Till Canceled orders, will stay current until either the customer ends it or the order itself expires and that could 60 to 120 days or more.

Things to Know

Learn How to Start An Online Business For FREE:
www.lacobizonlinebusiness.com

- A limit order may provide a guaranteed price if an order gets executed but total fulfillment of an order is not guaranteed, neither is partial fulfillment or whether the order is fulfilled at all. A limit order will be placed on the basis of first-come-first-served and that is only after all market orders are completed and provided the stock price remains inside your parameters long enough for the trade to be executed.

- Limit orders may result in higher commissions than market orders do. If a limit order cannot be fully executed in one go or inside of one day, it can spill over into the next day, and as many days as required to fill it – that equals more commission for every day that the trade continues over. And, if the stock doesn't get to the level of your limit order before it expires no execution takes place.

Making money from stocks is not easy. It takes a good deal of practice and no small amount of research, not to mention the most important factor of all – time. One last word of warning – never, ever invest any more money than you can comfortably afford to lose.

Learn How to Start An Online Business For FREE:
www.lacobizonlinebusiness.com

Drop Shipping

When you start your online business, one of the most important factors is actually having a product to sell. Without them, you really don't have a business. So, how do you go about getting these products? Where you do look for them? How do you even know that they are going to sell? Perhaps more importantly, how do you get these products to the customers who buy them?

The word of Internet business is huge and somewhere you will find the answers to all your questions. How about creating your own product to sell? Although that can take a lot of time and be costly. You could go to a manufacturer and purchase in bulk and then send them out to all those customers who buy them. That is also a very expensive option and you are also risking the investment of money in a stock with no guarantee of sales.

But there is one solution that can get you around all of this and it makes starting up a business a whole lot easier. That solution is called drop shipping and it is sweeping the online business world by a huge storm right now. Starting a drop shipping business is one of the easiest and fastest ways to go and let's not forget that it carries the lowest risk of all.

We'll look at how drop shipping businesses get started, how it works and what you need to know before you start one.

Starting the Drop Shipping Business

There are various estimates but according to industry watchers, around 20 to 30% of retailers who operate online use drop shipping. That it makes it a business model that is well and truly proven and a good route to go down. After all, if Amazon can successfully use drop shipping then why can't you?

Learn How to Start An Online Business For FREE: www.lacobizonlinebusiness.com

When you use drop shipping, you sell any product you want, regardless of niche. Even better, there is no need to get involved in all the problems faced by traditional business, including:

- Product storage. Purchasing large numbers of products, paying to store them and so on.

- Packaging and shipping. Another expensive by-product of business, not to mention the time it takes to package up the orders and then head for the post office to get them all sent. That kind of business is not scalable by any stretch of the imagination.

The most important factor – there is no need to put up any money upfront for wholesale product purchases that you can't guarantee being able to sell.

Running a drop shipping business means you avoid all of this and there is no risk to any capital either. Let's take a look at how it all works.

How Drop Shipping Works

When you get involved in drop shipping, you get together with a distributor or wholesaler that actually offers the service and not all do so you will need to do your homework. All the marketing is handled by you – your website or blog together with a shopping cart or you could use Amazon or Shopify for virtual storefronts. You fill your website with content, you take care of the email and social media marketing and you contact customers and leads. You let them know about your products, you tell them how your products will solve a problem they have. You make the sale.

Learn How to Start An Online Business For FREE:
www.lacobizonlinebusiness.com

Then the drop shipper will come in. They hold the inventory, they package the goods up and the send them out. When the orders come in you send them to the drop shipper and you pay the wholesale price. You can do this by emails, through a spreadsheet, even by submitting them online and they fulfill it.

There are fees. How much is going to depend on what the product is but it is usually a small handling fee of $2 to $5 per product, on top of the wholesale price and the shipping price and that can add up.

However, making a profit is still perfectly possible even though your margins are a bit slimmer. You can raise your prices if you want to raise that margin but be aware of going too far – you could lose your customers. And there is always room for negotiation as far as handing fees go with your drop shipper.

Do keep in mind – there is no risk to your cash up front. You only pay the fee if the product sells.

What Is Suitable For Drop Shipping?

All online businesses want to be involved in something that is trendy, where there is plenty of interest and lots of people buying. Best-case, you should choose an area you are interested in for your niche. If you are already passionate about a subject or a product then you will find it so much easier to market it and your enthusiasm will show through. And you get the added bonus that you actually enjoy doing this and that is enough to keep your motivation up.

You will be pleased to learn that just about every type of product can be drop shipped. There are companies that work with all markets, all niches, all types of product; all you need to do is

Learn How to Start An Online Business For FREE: www.lacobizonlinebusiness.com

find the one you want. Take a look at the large marketplaces online, like Amazon and eBay; here, you will find the products that are trending and that's a good place to start. Take a look at social media, see what is trending there; what's in the news, what everyone is talking about.

A big tip for you – think about the season. If its holiday season, or football season, or any other big season, find a product that is related to it – it will sell better.

One of the biggest mistakes made when they start an online business is that if others are doing the same thing, there is the thought that the niche is far too competitive and there's no money to be made. That is so untrue – where there is competition there is a good market and with the right work, you can get your slice of that particular pie.

Choosing a Drop Shipper

You can't work with a drop shipper until you have chosen one and to do that, you need to put yourself in the shoes of a customer, working through the entire order process as they would. You want to know how easy ordering is, the length of time taken to ship, and how each drop shipper will deal with any customer issues and other problems that arise.

This also lets you see exactly what the product is like, what quality it is – at the end of the day, it's important that your customers are happy with what they order. Some drop shipping companies will send you a free product so you can evaluate it or they will sell it to you at cost price.

If you have a specific niche and have previously used similar products, test it out for yourself. Use the product, study it

Learn How to Start An Online Business For FREE: www.lacobizonlinebusiness.com

closely, see whether it does what it should do. How is it made? Is it a quality product? Have a look at reviews online to see what others say about it.

If you don't have that niche, ask a friend to try the product and also do your homework as far as online reviews go. Look for forums to see if there are any comments, check Facebook, Twitter and other social media platforms. In short, do plenty of research.

If you know the product, you will find it easier to sell because you can market it far more effectively.

Some of the top drop shipping companies and directories in operation today are:

- Dropship Direct
- Oberlo
- Sunshine Wholesale
- Worldwide Brands

Alternatively, run a simple Google search for drop shippers and see what comes up.

Questions to Ask

Going into partnership with a drop shipper is a fantastic way of getting going with an online business without having to risk too much money upfront. And it makes running the business simple too because you don't have fork out for products that may not sell and you don't have to store them. Nor do you have to worry about packaging and shipping.

Learn How to Start An Online Business For FREE: www.lacobizonlinebusiness.com

However, you shouldn't be too quick to hand your business to just any old company; not all of them are reputable and you are risking your business before it even gets going. To help you find the right drop shipper, there are some questions you need to ask them:

- When an order has been placed, how long will it take to process it and ship it? (this is where it helps to go through the order process yourself, or get a friend to do it for you)

- What shipping methods do you offer? This is an important question if the drop shipping company are overseas and are doing international shipping. Do they make use of FedEx, UPS or other similar services? Can orders be sent by overnight shipping? Or do they just use the US Postal Service?

- Is there a tracking system in place so that customers can see exactly where their order is in the process and can it be tracked once shipped? Most customers want this so it's an important question.

- What do they do in the event that a shipment gets lost? You need to know so you can help your customers even though the issue is out of your control. Customer service is ultimately your problem so are shipments that go missing going to be down to you in terms of cost?

- Do they offer any guarantees or warranties with the product or is it a manufacturer warranty only? What if the customer doesn't like it? Do they have a return policy in place? What if the product fails after a short time? You don't want your customers to feel as though you are taking advantage of them so you need to ensure that your

Learn How to Start An Online Business For FREE: www.lacobizonlinebusiness.com

drop shipper offers a service that matches with what you promise your customers. It's you selling the product at the end of the day!

Do some online research about the drop shipping company too. Again, head to social media, forums, look for reviews and blogs. If a drop shipper has a bad reputation you will soon see it.

Drop shipping is one of the best and easiest ways to get your online business off the ground. The risk is low because you don't need to pay out a great deal up front and you don't have to store inventory either. And all the delivery details are taken care of by the drop shipper too.

All you have to do is pick your niche, set up your store and start marketing. If things work out you can always expand your store or add another niche. It's your choice but, done right, you can bring in a healthy income.

Learn How to Start An Online Business For FREE:
www.lacobizonlinebusiness.com

Shopify

Started in 2006 by a young German in Canada, as a small e-commerce store selling snowboards, Shopify is now the top tool for many who want a digital storefront. It is responsible for over half a million online stores, employment of over 3000 people and sales totaling well over $60 billion. Why wouldn't you choose it as your online store?

How it Works

Shopify is one of the easiest ways for anyone to start an online store and manage it. Full customer support is available, including helping store owners to branch out to other channels, such as Facebook, Amazon and eBay, plenty of support contact options, including online live chat and technical support.

Setting up Your Shop

Shopify has made it dead easy for you to start your store and, to help you decide if it is right for you, they even give you 14 days to try it for free. Let's build a store:

- First, you need a Shopify account so go to www.shopify.com and click on the Start Free Trial button

- Complete the details and click on Create Your Store Now. Do make sure that the name of your store is unique; if not, Shopify will want you to choose another – have a few written down, just in case.

- Next you will be asked to provide more details, including address, your country, a telephone number and so on. Do so and move on

Learn How to Start An Online Business For FREE:
www.lacobizonlinebusiness.com

- Now tell Shopify what products you are intending to sell, if you know at this point. If you just want to try Shopify, see how it works before you take the leap, click on the Do You Have Products menu and chose I'm Just Playing Around and, in the What Will You Sell menu, click I'm Not Sure.

- Click on I'm Done when you are finished.

The next step is to set up your shop and, once signup is complete, you will be redirected to your admin dashboard. Here, you can customize what you want, upload any products you have and set up your shipping and payments section. This is all self-explanatory so have a play around with everything and get it set up how you want it.

Choosing a Theme

You want some kind of thee so your storefront looks great and matches with the products you are selling. Shopify has a theme store and every theme included will be fully supported by the developers, and each comes with a modifications list, which means you can change things without having to write code. If you choose a premium theme, you get extra modifications but there are plenty of great-looking free ones to choose from. If you wanted to make a lot of changes to any theme and you are proficient in coding, you can go into the CSS and HTML but you can also hire one of the Shopify experts if you want to do that as well.

Let's choose a theme:

- Login to your Shopify account and go to the Theme Store

Learn How to Start An Online Business For FREE:
www.lacobizonlinebusiness.com

- Here, there are more than 180 different themes to choose from, and that includes a load of free ones. Filter by paid, free, features, industry, and so on to choose your theme.

- Once you have decided on one, click the sample image that comes with it. Now you will see some more details about the theme, such as how responsive it is, whether it works on mobile devices and so on. You can also see reviews from other store owners as to what they think of it

- Click on View Demo and you can see the theme in action. If there are different styles you can see all of them by clicking on each one

- When you have found the theme you want, click on the green button and confirm your selection

- Click on Publish as My Shop's Theme – if you are not completely sure it's the right one, it doesn't matter; you can change it later.

- Once your theme has been installed, Shopify will tell you and ask you if you want to go to Your Theme Manager. This will show you your themes, including any that you picked previously and uninstalled.

As we said earlier, most themes let you make a few changes that can change how your store looks; this means you can have something quite unique, something that doesn't look like every other store out there.

- Go to your admin screen and click on Themes – look in the left menu. Your theme will show up at the top inside a box and you will also see a pair of buttons. The one with

Learn How to Start An Online Business For FREE: www.lacobizonlinebusiness.com

three dots contains basic changes you can make to your settings; click on this and then click on the option to Duplicate your theme – the duplicate is the one you should work on until you have your changes correct; that way, if anything goes wrong the duplicate can be deleted and you can start again.

- Click the second button, this is customizing the theme. On this page you will see all the functionality of the store so have a play around with the settings and test it all out, see just what your site can do.

Some of the features you will find are:

- Uploading new logos
- Uploading slides if you have a carousel on your homepage
- Adding functionality to product pages
- Deciding how many items show up on each line
- Colors
- Fonts

On some of the themes you will also find the option to change how elements are positioned on the page, such as products, and whether you want to show social media buttons.

Adding Products

Provided you have some products ready to upload, you can go ahead and do it now:

- From your dashboard, go to the left and choose Products

Learn How to Start An Online Business For FREE:
www.lacobizonlinebusiness.com

- Click the Add a Product button – top corner of your screen

- Add all the detail you can about the products and when you do this, think about SEO – the name of the product, use keywords in the description, and the URL. Put in as much as you can to help your customers know about this product

- Next, you can upload the images of the products; it doesn't matter what order you do this in because you can rearrange them later. Your images are very important to your sales so make sure they are the best images; use close-ups if you have special or unique features that you want to show off. And make sure all your images are of the same dimensions.

- Click on Save Product after you have done each one.

You can also set up collections, which are just groups of similar products. For example, a customer visiting your store might search for:

- Women's/men's/children's clothes
- Lamps
- Rugs
- Cushions
- Sale items
- Specific colors or sizes
- Seasonal products

Learn How to Start An Online Business For FREE: www.lacobizonlinebusiness.com

You can place individual products into multiple collections and these are then displayed, normally, on your home page. This lets customers complete their searches easily without needing to search your entire store.

When new collections are added, it's up to you how you populate it with products and you have two choices:

- **Manual** – add products and remove them manually
- **Automatic** – set up specific conditions that allow for automatic inclusion of products that meet set criteria

Payments

You will need a payment gateway so that your customers can pay for their purchases. Two three things are important when you look for one – the price, the commission charges, and what features they have. You will need to compare several and choose only the ones that meet your requirements. These are important features to consider:

- **Transaction Fees** – some gateways will retain a fee per transaction, either a flat fee or a percentage. This is their fee for you using their gateway and you will need to consider these fees in conjunction with expected sales.
- **Cards** – you must determine which credit and debit cards the gateway accepts for payment. All of them will take Mastercard and Visa, some will take American Express and more and more are also starting to accept PayPal, which is an important factor in your decision.
- **Checkout Offsite** – some gateways prefer to provide their own form and accept the payment on their own

Learn How to Start An Online Business For FREE:
www.lacobizonlinebusiness.com

servers; the customer will be redirected from your website to theirs and, once the payment is done, they get sent back to a confirmation page provided by you. This gives you a little more control over the process.

From November 2018, stores in the US and the UK gained the option to use Shopify payments. Depending on which plan you opt for, you may also be able to save money on transaction fees, which are added over the top of the Shopify transaction fees. :

- **Basic Plan** – 2.4% plus a small fee per transaction
- **Professional Plan** – 2.1% plus a small fee per transaction
- **Unlimited Plan** – 1.8% plus a small fee per transaction

Whether you upgrade to take advantage of those rates will depend on how many transactions your shop gets every month.

To choose between Shopify Payments and another Gateway, go to Settings>Payments and click on either Complete Shopify Payments or Enable Payment Gateway.

Let's Go Live

There is a bit more to do before your site can go live, mainly adding company details and deciding on shipping and taxes.

- Make sure you have completed all of your business details and enable the option for Google Analytics; this is a great tool for helping track your visitors. Now we need to sort out taxes:
- On your admin page, click on Products

Learn How to Start An Online Business For FREE: www.lacobizonlinebusiness.com

- Choose a product and click on it

- Click on Inventory and Variants, near the bottom of the page

- Beside the product variant is an edit link; click on this and a dialog box will open

- Check the boxes next to Requires Shipping and Charge Taxes if these are to be included with each product. Some stores won't need this if they are selling digital goods or services but physical products most likely will do.

- Lastly, if a product needs to be shipped, put its weight, or an approximation, in the box provided.

Be aware of your shipping rates; if you don't provide sufficient choice or your rates are far too narrow you are likely to lose customers. Shopify calculates shopping rates based only on what you define on your admin shipping page:

- From your admin page, click on Settings>Shipping

- Go to the section for Shipping Rates and see if your rates are based on weight; adjust this to match the specifications of your product

Testing your order system is also important and to do that you can use the Bogus Gateway in Shopify for a transaction simulation:

- From your admin page, click on Settings>Payments

- If your enabled gateway is a credit card one, deactivate it before you go any further – Edit>Deactivate and then confirm.

Learn How to Start An Online Business For FREE:
www.lacobizonlinebusiness.com

- Go to the section for Accept Credit Cards and click on Select a Credit Card Gateway

- In the list, click on Other>Bogus Gateway

- Click on Activate

- Head to your storefront and act like a customer, placing an order. When you get to Checkout, enter Bogus Gateway as your credit card name. For the card number, input 1 (a successful transaction), 2 (a failed transaction) or 3 (an exception, i.e. an issue with the card provider). Try each of these in turn to see what happens. For the CCV number put in any three numbers and the expiry date can be any date you like in the future.

You can also test using a real transaction. Reactivate your payment gateway and go through the process of purchasing a product and use real card details to complete it. Do make sure you cancel the order so you get refunded and don't have to pay any transaction fees.

Domain Name

To go live you need a domain name and you have two options here – buy one via Shopify and it gets added straight away. This option saves time because you don't need to worry about website hosting and you will usually pay between $9 and $14 per year. The second option is to buy a domain from a domain provider. These cost as little as $1.99 a year but they have one downside – retrieving the DNS records is down to you. Don't worry, I will show you how to do it.

- Purchase your domain through a third party

Learn How to Start An Online Business For FREE:
www.lacobizonlinebusiness.com

- Go to your Shopify admin page and click on Settings
- Click on Domains, click on Add An Existing Domain and input your domain name

Now we can update the DNS records:

- Log in to the domain registrar (where you purchased your domain name from)
- Change the records this way:
- The main A record or @ sign should be replaced with the IP address 23.227.38.32
- Either replace or add the www CName – it should read www.storename.myshopify.com (using your own Shopify store name – do not add the HTTP in front of it).
- Lastly, remove the password set on your store and it will go live – anyone will be able to access it.

Learn How to Start An Online Business For FREE: www.lacobizonlinebusiness.com

Amazon FBA

Fulfillment by Amazon is fast becoming a very popular model for online businesses and there is a very good reason for that. Although it is very much like the traditional eCommerce solution we are all familiar with, it differs in one way – rather than having to fulfill orders on an individual basis, Amazon will store all your products and they will fulfill every order, taking care of packaging and delivery.

Using Amazon FBA makes building your business very easy because you don't need to worry about storage, packaging, posting, and everything else that goes with that side of your business. Plus, if you use private labeling you can build up your own website and brand.

What is FBA?

With Amazon FBA, you can take advantage of the huge, stable network and the customer base that makes up the largest online marketplace in the world. As I mentioned, Amazon will take care of the storage of your products, fulfill all your orders, and they will even take care of the customer service side of things so you can concentrate on your marketing and selling efforts.

What this means for you is that, even with a new business, you can act as if it is a huge enterprise but without all the headaches that go with that. Typically with eCommerce, it's down to you to work out what the logistics are of getting products out to customers in a timely manner. With FBA, any Prime member will get their product within a couple of business days.

Another of the challenges you face with eCommerce is keeping an up to date inventory and listing other products, thus making things even more complex. All you need to do with FBA is send

Learn How to Start An Online Business For FREE:
www.lacobizonlinebusiness.com

all your products to Amazon and they will do the donkey work. That means you can add extra products without increasing your workload too much.

Creating an Account

Before you can even think about FBA, you need an Amazon seller account and you do this by visiting the Amazon website. In the footer of the website you will see an option that says Make Money with Us; click on this and then click on Sell on Amazon.

Here you can choose whether to go for a professional account or an individual one. If you go for Individual, you don't get charged the subscription fee every month but if your aim is to build up a business then you really should choose Professional. You get the first 30 days free and then it's $39.99 per month plus the selling fees.

Aside from that, it is quite easy to sign up; all the instructions are on the screen.

Opportunities and Private Label

You can make use of FBA in several different ways but private labeling appears to be the most common use. The idea behind this is that you establish your own label or brand, give it to your product and sell it via the Amazon marketplace.

The most important thing about this is doing your research on Amazon products. Why is this important? If you go into a product category that is not very popular and you price your product above what your competitors sell for, you stand to lose out. If you take the time out to do your research, find a product that is popular, research the competition, look at the reviews for

Learn How to Start An Online Business For FREE: www.lacobizonlinebusiness.com

the products, and identify one product that you could sell cheaper or make better, that's where you need to start.

Retail arbitrage is another popular selling method through Amazon. This is the process of purchasing a product that is already branded and flipping it for profit on Amazon. This is a great way of making a bit of money in the short term.

When you go into private labeling you will need some capital. When you order private label products expect to fork out a few thousand dollars; expensive but, if your aim is to build up an asset that you can sell later then this is the way to go.

Your supplier is another piece of your puzzle. If you have no inventory, you can't make any sales and that means no money so it's up to you to make sure there is little delay between you placing the stock order and it being delivered and that comes down to choosing the right supplier.

Tips to Grow Your FBA Business

- **Follow your passion.** If it's something you enjoy doing, you are going to be more successful because you will stick to it. That's why it is important that you find a category and a product that you are interested in and excited about.

- **Offer more products** – although you need to do proper research for any product that you offer, you should offer more than just one product. If you don't, your business becomes dependent on that one product and has a higher chance of failure when sales start to fall.

- **Improve your BSR** – your Best Seller Rank is one of the most important metrics, not just for your sales but for

Learn How to Start An Online Business For FREE: www.lacobizonlinebusiness.com

your customers too. And, if you ever decide to sell your business, the higher your BSR, the easier it will be to sell.

- **Build your website** – the best way to build up your offerings under your private label is to build up your website. Make it a professional one, dedicated to your business.

- **Become an Amazon Associate** – if you join the Amazon affiliate program you stand a much better chance of increasing your product offerings and your revenue.

Amazon FBA Potential for Earning

So, how much can you earn using Amazon FBA? That's not easy to answer because it all depends on you but there are some examples to consider. Spencer Haws, the owner of Niche Pursuits, reported earnings of $40,000 in the first month of his FBA business. Chris Guthrie, the owner of UpFuel, reported $3,000 in the first month while the founder of Feedbackz, James Amazio, went from nothing to $earning $50,000 a month, all within 8 months of starting.

These may not be typical results but they are proof that, if you put in the time and effort, you can use FBA to build up a fantastic business.

5 More Ways to Grow Your FBA Business

Keep Within Your Strengths

Do you have a real passion for the products you are selling? Have you any resources or connections within your chosen industry that you can use to help grow your own business? One

Learn How to Start An Online Business For FREE: www.lacobizonlinebusiness.com

of the best ways to make money and maintain motivation is to sell something that you have an interest in.

If you need to hire staff, do look for those that share your passions; it's the quickest way to grow a business, hiring staff who are genuinely interested in what you do.

Lastly, make sure you and your supplier have a good relationship. It doesn't hurt to ask if there is any way they can help you to cut your costs or get a better quality of products. Make sure they know that you in this long-term, it isn't a five-minute wonder. If they won't listen to you, see about finding a new supplier that will.

Tracking and Recording

When you own an FBA business, always make sure your financial data is tracked and recorded right from the very first day. Doing this lets you see exactly what is going on and whether the business is worth the effort. Plus, if you do have a successful business and you decide, one day, that you want to sell it, it works in your favor if you have all the financial details to hand. Record everything, even if you don't think it is valuable data.

Another thing you need to see is whether your business is cost efficient or not. Once all your expenses and fees have been paid, are you still turning a profit? Most of the time, FBA businesses see an approximate gross margin of around 15 to 20% - is your business up there with that?

Most people who start an FBA business do not ask themselves any of these questions. If you want to manage your cash flow properly and accurately, you need to track your key indicators for performance – ratio for inventory to sales, turnover of

Learn How to Start An Online Business For FREE:
www.lacobizonlinebusiness.com

inventory, what your gross margin ROI (return on investment) is, and so on.

Have a Bigger Online Presence with a Website

If there is one major issue about using Amazon as a platform for your business, it's that you don't actually own it. And because you don't own Amazon, you can't access any of their customer data. That causes a problem because this is the kind of data that is vital to the scaling of your business over time.

There are a few tools available that you can use to get access to that data but one of the best ways to build up customer data of your own is to build a website, marketing your own business. If you do your marketing and advertising properly, you can direct your own traffic to the website and you can collect email addresses. With those, you can run targeted email campaigns, passing on the news about special offers, discounts, and new products and so on. Even better, that email address list is yours, a great asset for those who intend to sell on their businesses later down the line.

Make Use of Paid Advertising

SEO is an ongoing strategy, one that you should be ever-conscious of. When you don't own the platform you are selling from, you can't even begin to optimize it. The very best way to start putting the word out about your business is to use paid advertising. Using this means you don't need to make a lot of changes to your website or fill it with large amounts of content that you may not have the time to push out. By using paid advertising, you can reduce the costs of acquiring customers by up to 80%.

Learn How to Start An Online Business For FREE: www.lacobizonlinebusiness.com

However, for paid advertising to be successful, you will need to run a few tests. It doesn't matter if you think you know your business inside out; the chances of you picking on a sound, winning strategy first time out are slim. Try the following:

- A/B split test – test different images to see which ones work and which ones don't – remember, your audience will always see images before they see the text.

- Split-test the copy – the same with images, test different kinds of copy to see which ones draw the most positive attention.

- Gather data on your audience – build up an email list and use tools to help you understand them. A good one to use is Amazon MWS Customer/Order Export.

- Use retarget methods. Capture your buyers when they go offsite to try to tempt them back.

The best combination of paid advertising is Amazon PPC and email marketing but look into all the forms of paid ads you can find and do weigh up the pros, cons and cost before you dive in.

Improve your BSR

This is something we mentioned earlier; while there isn't a guide to go by for improving your best-seller rank, it is one of the most important metrics to measure your business by. What you are aiming for is more sales than your nearest competition but if this proves too challenging, consider that you can always change your products and move into a less competitive area if you need to. Make sure your customers are offered the very best products and the very best customer service; you want positive reviews, not negativity, because this will have an effect on your BSR.
Learn How to Start An Online Business For FREE:
www.lacobizonlinebusiness.com

It isn't hard to start an FBA business and it doesn't cost much either; the hardest part is in scaling your business and that is where too many new online businesses fail. Use the resources and connections you have; make the most of your expertise, of the passion you bring to your subject and you do stand a much better chance of succeeding. And don't forget to use what tools that Amazon offers; these are invaluable to you.

Learn How to Start An Online Business For FREE:
www.lacobizonlinebusiness.com

Publishing on Amazon

The final business model revolves around writing your own eBooks and publishing them using Amazon KDP – Kindle Direct Publishing. Obviously, your first step is to write your book and get it ready to sell. KDP is the first port of call for most authors who want to publish online. For some, it will be the only retailer they can or will submit their books to.

Setting Up

- Your first step is to sign up for an Amazon KDP account – you will need an Amazon account for this. Go to http://kdp.amazon.com and sign up. You can use your current Amazon login details or you can set up another account just for using with KDP, it's your choice but you may only have one KDP account.

- Sign into your KDP account once you have set it up and start filling in your details. First, you need to add some banking details and you will likely be asked to sign in again, just to confirm you are who you say you are. Make sure you fill in the correct name and address and then click the button that says Complete Tax Information. Answer the questions that come up on the screen so that Amazon can track all payments from a tax point of view.

- Now click on Add a Bank Account – complete the name of your bank, the routing number and the account number so that Amazon can pay your royalties to you. You can't get around this step if you want to publish on Amazon and if you refuse to provide your banking details, they will refuse to publish your book.

Learn How to Start An Online Business For FREE:
www.lacobizonlinebusiness.com

- Once all your data has been entered, choose how you want to be paid. Your account will be set, by default, to be paid in your local currency by check but you can choose to be paid by electronic transfer in your currency or in US dollars.

Publish Your Book

Once all your details have been entered, you are ready to publish your hard work to the world.

- In your KDP account, go to the top of your screen and click on Bookshelf and then on Add New Title. Complete the form with the relevant details – the title of the book, subtitle if there is one. A book description, relevant keywords and so on. The keywords are the words that people will use when they search for your book. Make sure everything is completed and then you can move on.

- The next step is to upload your book cover and then the book itself. Book covers are important and many people fork out the money to have one designed for them – this is a good idea because the cover is the first thing people see – if it isn't good, few people will read the book.

Happy with the way it looks? Go to the bottom of the page where you can add other details; an ISBN number if you have one (you don't need this for an eBook but if you want one, you can purchase on online); the name of your publisher if you have one, and so on. Complete all the details that you can, make sure everything is correct and then click the Save and Continue button at the bottom of the page. In a few seconds, you will reach the last step – pricing.

Learn How to Start An Online Business For FREE:
www.lacobizonlinebusiness.com

- First of all, you need to make a decision – are you offering your eBook for sale solely through Amazon, for at least 90 days? It's the best option so click on the KDP Select enrolment button if you are happy to stick with it.

- Next you need to tell Amazon what rights you have to sell the book, be it in specific countries or worldwide.

- Now choose which royalty share you want to sign up to. There are a few variables but it comes down to this – f you want the full 70% royalty, less a fee of $0.015 per megabyte, the book should be priced between $2.99 and $9.99. If you want your book priced higher, or you want to get around the fee for transferring, choose the option for 35% royalties.

- Now it's time to set your price. Amazon can automatically convert your price form USD to other countries or you can click Other Marketplaces and set a price for each country. It is better to do this because converted prices tend to look a bit odd.

- There is just a little more to complete. First, is your book solely an eBook or is there a print version? If there is, chose the option for Matchbook – this will give purchasers of the print version the option of purchasing the eBook version at a huge discount, so long as the price is 50 or less than the print book.

- If you choose the Lending option, buyers will be able to end their copy of your book to another customer; this is an excellent way of encouraging people to purchase. A word of note – if you opt for 70% royalty rate, this is mandatory.

Learn How to Start An Online Business For FREE:
www.lacobizonlinebusiness.com

Are you ready? Because now is the best bit. Click on Publish Your eBook and, within a few hours, your book will be available on the Kindle platform on Amazon. You will be redirected back to your bookshelf and you will note that the book title is greyed out. This means, until your book has been accepted and published by Amazon, you cannot edit anything. This is why it is important to make sure everything is correct before you hit that button. Once it has been published you can change what you like so if it doesn't seem to be selling well, change a few things and see what works.

You are now an independent publisher on the Amazon platform.

Pros of Self-Publishing

- **The Potential for Income is Good** – when you publish your own book, you get a first-hand glimpse into exactly what it takes and that should give you an idea of how expensive it would be through a traditional publisher. Each task that is involved is carried out by a different person and they must be paid; the more people you pay, the less profit there is for you. Go down the traditional route and your share of the profit will typically be no more than 15%.

- **More Control** – many agents won't entertain unique ideas or visions but with self-publishing the world is your oyster. Experiment how you want, go the route you want to go, choose your own editors, designers, proofreaders, and so on. The book will be a vision made 100% from what you want it to be.

- **Publishing Is Much Quicker** – publishing houses tend to lock you into their own schedule and how fast it

Learn How to Start An Online Business For FREE:
www.lacobizonlinebusiness.com

moves will depend on their resources. Publish your own book and it can be out there in just a few hours.

The Cons of Self-Publishing

- **You Do All The Work** – you may have control but everything, every last little job, is down to you. You can't work to someone else's schedule, use their staff, or anything like that. If this is your first time at self-publishing that might prove challenging.

- **Lack of Credibility** – because some self-published authors churn out a load of rubbish, all self-published authors tend to be lumped into the same group. It will take a lot of hard work if you are to get your book to stand out and prove that you should not all be tarred with the same brush.

- **Capital is Down to you** – when you have the support of a publishing house, the money is down to them. Of course they will recoup it from you over time if your book sells but you don't need to worry. If you self-publish, it's all down to you. You must hope and pray that your book sells enough to at least replace what you paid, if not make a healthy profit.

It is down to you but if you take the time, do your homework and market it properly, eBooks can bring in a decent, steady revenue. And, if the first one sells well, you have the option of writing a follow-up.

Learn How to Start An Online Business For FREE: www.lacobizonlinebusiness.com

Part 3: Running Your Business Successfully

Now you know all about setting up your own online business, what it entails and we looked at some of the best business models that you can choose from too. It's time for the final part – running your business successfully. This last section is a mixture of facts and tips that will help you to get off and running and follow your dream to success.

21 Secrets to Online Business Success

There are many misconceptions, half-truths and downright lies about what it really takes to run an online business successfully and even business owners with years of experience seriously underestimate how much time and energy is needed, not to mention skill. If you really want to succeed in your online business, take note of and understand these facts so you know exactly what you are getting into:

- **Online businesses tend to grow very fast.**

While you can't expect to be a complete success overnight, although some have achieved that fame, it is quite rare for an online business to go beyond two years without seeing success. This is truer if you have centered yourself firmly in a highly competitive niche. If you get to a year or two into your business and success isn't coming then it's time to sit back and take a long hard look at your business model.

- **You can save time and money by using some fantastic tools**

Here's your challenge – find one highly successful online business that hasn't used and still does use upwards of 5 to 10 online tools to help them run it. It's true to say that if you don't make use of the tools on offer you are likely to fail; these tools are developed for a reason – to make life easier for you, increase

Learn How to Start An Online Business For FREE: www.lacobizonlinebusiness.com

the success chances of your business and help you to automate parts of the business. There are thousands to choose from – social media, email marketing, online invoicing and so on. Find the ones that work for you and use them well to save you time, money and increase business productivity.

- **Knowing when to throw the towel in**

This is one of the biggest keys to being a success. Yes, everywhere you look, you will find advice and quotes that tell you never to give up but sometimes cutting your losses and going back to the beginning is the best way. Many successful online business owners have tried several models before they gained the success they wanted and knowing when it's time to give up and move on is key to your eventual success. It doesn't have to be your entire business; if a strategy, campaign or even an employee is not working out, ditch it and move on. If you have trusted friends or colleagues, listen to what they say – you can't always be on top of everything and if they tell you something isn't working, it just might be true.

- **Online businesses outsource**

Outsourcing is becoming very common and David Ogilvy, a famous tycoon in the advertising business, once said, "Hire people who are better than you and leave them to get on with the job". You can't know everything and you can't be everything. If you want to be in with a competitive chance, outsource anything that you can't do and anything that you really don't enjoy doing. There are loads of freelancers who can design websites, logos, draw up a marketing campaign, and so on and they are not expensive. The cost is small compared to the success it could bring you and it leaves you free to concentrate on doing what you love. One word of advice – don't leave your entire business

Learn How to Start An Online Business For FREE:
www.lacobizonlinebusiness.com

in the hands of freelancers – you might not have a business to come back to.

- **Social media is a huge weapon in the online business world**

It's really quite simple; an online business cannot be successfully run without using social media. Almost two-thirds of all referrals traffic to some of the most successful businesses comes via a social media platform. If you aren't using it, you cannot get your message out to new customers; not only that, it's also easier to stay in touch with existing customers so get on and set up your social media accounts.

- **Successful businesses know and accept that passive income really isn't that passive.**

So many people believe that you can run a successful online business by doing the bare minimum, spending the rest of your day lounging about doing nothing. Yes, online businesses do provide a lot more flexibility than a standard job but passive income really isn't all that passive. You can automate certain parts of your business and you can let it run without being too hands on but you still need to oversee everything, you still need to manage everything and, if you are running a blog, you still need to upload regular content. Your social media campaigns won't run themselves either!

- **Online business owners are focused on the big picture**

Not everyone will be able to run an online business; it simply doesn't suit everyone, If you are one of those who likes to focus on detail rather than on plans, goals, trends, etc., it may not be

Learn How to Start An Online Business For FREE:
www.lacobizonlinebusiness.com

the best choice for you. For an online business to be successful, you must be able to focus on everything.

- **They know what value they are providing**

You cannot possibly compete if you undervalue your service or product. Yes, to start with, it might be rather tempting to get a jump on the competition by undercutting them but the best option is to set prices that you can sustain and that will still make you money long into the future. If you do opt to go for a lower price to start with, you must tell customers that this is a short-term offer and that prices will go up!

- **Successful businesses start growing their email lists on day one**

There is no getting away from the fact that email marketing is one of the most important of all business strategies and for the online business, it is critical. Research shows that a properly done email campaign results in a much better rate of click-through, more engagement and higher sales figures. It has been suggested that this type of campaign will give you a much higher return on investment than any other online campaign so start from the very first day, get your list on the go and start seeing the real benefits.

- **Successful businesses solve a problem – a real one**

Success for an online business requires you to find your niche and find a genuine need in it. Ask yourself what problem you can solve? What need can you fulfill? Does your product or your service do that? If not, ask yourself if there is a way to make it happen or decide whether to move on to something else.

Learn How to Start An Online Business For FREE: www.lacobizonlinebusiness.com

- **Online businesses make themselves different from the others**

The e-commerce market is beyond huge. Conservative estimates say that it is a multi-billion dollar market that is spread across more than 12 million stores online. That makes it critical that you differentiate yourself from the others otherwise you won't get a slice of that pie, probably not even the leftover crumbs.

- **They understand that quality content is valuable**

At one time, it used to be optional to take part in content marketing. Not any more. If you can't produce a regular stream of high-quality, relevant, up to date and simply amazing content, you won't even get off the starting line.

- **They are 100% in it**

There are those who think that it is easy to build an incredibly successful business in the couple of spare hours they have each day. Most of their focus is on their standard job and the online business gets looked at when they have five minutes. You cannot build a truly successful business like this. Sure you can start out that way but eventually you will have to accept that it needs more time and effort. It isn't a hobby; give it the attention it needs and it will grow into a proper business.

- **They listen to what their customers are saying**

Never underestimate what value your customers provide in the growth of your business. Listen to what they say; take their suggestions on-board, even try some of them out. You don't know what might work and what won't until you do try. Ask them for their ideas and suggestions, ask them what products they want to see. Nothing ventured, nothing gained, as they say.

Learn How to Start An Online Business For FREE:
www.lacobizonlinebusiness.com

- **Their business is their passion**

It isn't easy to make a living online and running a business is tough stuff. That is why is it all-important that you choose something you have a passion for. You need to ask yourself if you can see yourself still running this business in 5 years' time – if not, it isn't the business for you so you will need to find another direction to go in, one that you have a real passion for.

- **SEO is all-important to them**

More than 80% of online marketers believe that SEO is getting more and more effective as time passes. One of the most important things for any business is getting high search engine rankings as this is where a large portion of your traffic is going to come from. Learn all you can about SEO and apply it; if you really don't understand it, this may be something you should consider outsourcing.

- **Successful businesses don't wait for perfection before they move**

You don't need to know every little thing about running a business before you start one, although some knowledge is preferred. You also don't need everything to be 100% perfect. Go for it and improve as you go; wait too long and your opportunity will be gone snapped up by another entrepreneur.

- **They accept that the golden goose is out of reach**

There isn't any magic formula for success at an online business but too many owners still waste so much time, effort and money on trying to find that one strategy that will throw them int the limelight and achieve success immediately. It doesn't exist. The only golden goose is this – hard work and persistence. Forget Learn How to Start An Online Business For FREE: www.lacobizonlinebusiness.com

about that one strategy; get your head down, sweat over the hard work and the rewards will come in.

- **Successful businesses have a proper plan**

There is another myth about the online business that I really need to bust – people rarely just stumble over your website by accident, buy a load of stuff and fill your bank account up. It doesn't happen with a physical business and it certainly won't happen with an online one. Sure, a very small percentage of your customers will be those who found you by mistake but what you will really benefit from is having a proper, written business plan and a properly written marketing strategy.

- **They don't allow failure to knock them back**

Failure is a part of any business and it is one of the biggest learning curves too. What really counts is how you deal with failure. Do you let it knock you back or do you learn from it and move on. What if your SEO strategy simply isn't working? Go back to it, change your keywords. Is your content not working? Write better, in-depth, focused content. Whatever the failure is, don't let it get you down; hit straight back and find a better way.

- **They are true dominators of their niche**

If you learn only one thing from all this, it should be that you never bash your head against a brick wall by trying to be too competitive. Narrow down your niche instead, find that one industry subset where you can excel and work on dominating it. Take a business that offers storage for Christmas trees. The obvious focus would the industry that focuses on holiday decorations. Instead, focus on the storage aspect. Offer cheaper and better storage facilities than anyone else. Build from there

Learn How to Start An Online Business For FREE: www.lacobizonlinebusiness.com

and leave the big boys playing at the top by themselves – you will catch them up.

Learn How to Start An Online Business For FREE:
www.lacobizonlinebusiness.com

More Mistakes to Avoid

When you start your online business, you focus on building up your online presence and credibility, on fulfilling needs and solving a problem. What really goes into making it a huge success is more than that, though, because although the entry barriers are low, most people will fail because of mistakes that, when they think back on them, were common sense. They overestimate what their profits might be, or they try to be too much form the word go. Let's look at another 10 very common mistakes that you should avoid when you are trying to start your business online.

You don't have a plan

Really and truthfully, you should have a proper business plan, all drawn up and written down for you to refer to. However, any plan is better than no plan. So many potential owners see drawing up a business plan as a piece of homework that they have no interest in and they seriously underestimate how helpful a plan can be. There are several things that you really need to know to get started – who are your customers? What products or services are you selling? What do you think the value of those products or services is, what are people prepared to pay? You also need to know exactly how much money you have to play with, where you are going to invest it and what you are prepared to pay for.

You sweat the small stuff

The most important thing is actually getting your business off and running. This might seem to be somewhat obvious but to many new business owners spend too much time on the small details and forget about the bigger picture. When you spend too

Learn How to Start An Online Business For FREE: www.lacobizonlinebusiness.com

much time worrying about the design of your business logo or business cards, you are wasting valuable time that could and should be spent on the tasks that are going to push your business up the ranks. Hire a freelancer to do your logo and cards; you need to focus on actually running the business.

You don't worry enough about money

Optimism is a good thing but not where money is concerned. It doesn't grow on trees and the chances are, unless you have a never-ending stream of the stuff, the money will run out before your business starts to make any. You must always know exactly how much money you can invest in the business, know exactly what your burn rate is and ensure that you have a way of getting more money before it's too late. Too many owners scrabble around to find more when it's already far too late. This is why you should have a financial plan in place, listing your milestones, how much money needs to be spent to get to those goals and when you are likely to need more.

You don't put enough value on your product or service

It doesn't matter whether you are selling a physical product, a digital product or an online service; it needs to be priced to make a decent profit while not being out of reach of most people. Consider what it costs to produce, especially where products are concerned – the cost of the materials, the labor, the time, and so on. Set it at a price that tops that, making you a profit and still being affordable. As things evolve, you can consider making changes to the price points – but only when the money is coming in steadily.

You don't pay attention to customer service

Learn How to Start An Online Business For FREE: www.lacobizonlinebusiness.com

Without customers, you do not have a business and with so much going on over the Internet now, it is all too easy to forget that those customers are still real people. Give them an experience they love and they'll come back. You must have a way of talking to your customers on your website, be it through email, live chat, even a phone number. And don't forget social media. If people follow your page or account, make sure you interact with them; don't forget about them because the human race is fickle – they will very quickly move on.

You give far too much away and get nothing back

One of the best ways to get yourself established is to offer freebies. Before your credibility is established, free products or services can entice customers to become return customers, particularly where services are on offer. However, give too much away and the cost can be far more than you can afford. Instead, think of something a customer can benefit from without it costing you too much – a free eBook, a guide, a webinar, a free recipe, and so on. Getting their name on your email list is important but not to the cost of your business. When you give too much away, some customers come to expect everything for free and won't stump up when you charge for it.

You have too many social media accounts

When you first start marketing it can be so tempting to sign up to every social media site going. After all, the more you can put the word around, the more visitors you will get, right? Wring. If you sign up to everything you will not have time to build quality contacts. Start with one or two, preferably Facebook followed by Pinterest if you are selling products. LinkedIn is great for building business brands and for repurposing your content.

Learn How to Start An Online Business For FREE:
www.lacobizonlinebusiness.com

Don't spread yourself too thin; time is of the essence and you can't possibly spend quality time on everything.

You hire the wrong people

When you first start hiring, it is important not to rush the process. It won't help you to scale your business if you hire the wrong people at the start. You need your hires to have the right skill set, the right business needs, the right attitude and the right personality that fits with your culture, not to mention the right commitment to furthering your business. Look for those people who possess the skills that you don't have and have the qualities that you respect and need. The first five people you hire will set the stage for the entire life of your business.

You underestimate the drive you need for success

No doubt you have read tons of stuff on how important it is to balance your work and home life. Forget it, at least for a year or so. You won't get those big ideas, those winning strategies when you are too busy counting and managing every minute. They definitely won't come to you when you are trying to do too many other things. You need to focus on one thing and one thing only; everything else should be pushed to the back of your mind.

You make the mistake of thinking that one size will fit everything

A product, a service, even a marketing strategy, may work for one company but that doesn't mean it will work for every company. You need to have a certain amount of skepticism when you read stuff, when you see successful companies touting one or two strategies. Test your own products and services using

Learn How to Start An Online Business For FREE: www.lacobizonlinebusiness.com

the minimum amount of risk in terms of money and resources and test out multiple strategies – see what works for you.

Learn How to Start An Online Business For FREE:
www.lacobizonlinebusiness.com

Scaling Your Business

It really isn't rocket science you know. Scaling your business online is easier than you might think. All you need to do is have a winning service or products and a solid ground to grow up from – from there, the only limits are you and your creativity. Here are five tips to help you scale your business:

Make it a doddle for customers to purchase your service or product:

How many websites have you visited where you have had to go through such a performance just to purchase something that you gave up halfway through? Too many to mention? This is one of the biggest problems with online businesses – some make it far too difficult for their customers to make their purchase and that is the easiest way to lose them – fast.

Test your own purchasing process for yourself. If it's too difficult, look at ways to reduce the steps. In all honesty, all your customers want to do is click and buy – think Amazon, eBay and all the other major online sellers.

Track every conversion that you can think of

You really do need to know your numbers – down to the last penny. How much is it costing you to generate your leads? If you don't know, your business is likely to fail. Two of the most important metrics that you must track are:

- **CPL** – Cost Per Lead – It is important that you know exactly what each of your lead forms costs to generate, be they phone calls or email submissions. What won't work is a blended CPL – you need to narrow things down as specifically as you can. If you can generate leads from

Learn How to Start An Online Business For FREE: www.lacobizonlinebusiness.com

emails for a dollar and it's costing you $10 to generate a phone lead but both have identical conversion rates, it would make sense to drop the phone calls and concentrate your efforts on email marketing.

- **CPS** – Cost Per Sale – never forget that every piece of data works together with the rest. Your CPL and your conversion rates, for example, will both work to determine what you are spending per sale. It should be common sense that if your CPS together with the cost of the products you sold is less then what you are bringing in through sales, then you are making a profit. But you need to go more in-depth than that. Where is the lowest possible CPS coming from? Is there any way to get more sales using that method so you can ditch a more expensive method?

You also need to look at the conversion rates on each of your landing pages and which sources are your best performers. You will never find that magic formula that you can set up and forget about, it just doesn't exist. You must be forever on top of things, looking for a way to optimize your business to get the best reward and the highest profit.

Highlight your specific expertise through the media

Scaling your online business can only be done if you are prepared to put your business and your brand out there for all to see. There are loads of ways that you can free exposure through the media, provided you are prepared to put the work in.

Get yourself registered with HARO – Help a Reporter Out. They have well over 30000 journalists who are all looking for that little bit of insight from industry experts and if you take the time

Learn How to Start An Online Business For FREE:
www.Iacobizonlinebusiness.com

and put the work in, you are likely to come across a number of excellent opportunities for exposure. You do need to be consistent to reap any reward from this, though.

Every day, HARO will send out three emails, each one bursting with opportunity. Many business owners will look at them for a couple of days and then forget about them if an opportunity doesn't throw itself at them straight away. Don't do this. Stick with it put in more effort to the responses you send. Every journalist will get hundreds of replies to their requests so it's up to you to make sure your stands out from all the rest. Later, I'll talk a bit more about press outreach as it can be one of the best SEO strategies you ever learn about.

Automate your email sequences for constant promotion and conversion

All businesses regardless of type can make good use of email automation. If you run a restaurant, for example, you could set up an email list that automatically sends coupons out for discounts and special offers on days when business is slow, just to boost foot traffic a little. Those who run an e-commerce store can use segmented lists to send offers out to customers based on what they have been looking at and/or purchased in the past.

If you are selling an information product, you can build up a list by capturing mail addresses and then use that list for automatically targeting prospects with discounts and information until they convert to a sale.

Email automation is much like any other marketing form; to get it right, you will have to split test extensively and constantly optimize but, when you get it right, email automation can be a

Learn How to Start An Online Business For FREE:
www.lacobizonlinebusiness.com

system that promotes your business, nurtures leads and converts all day long, even when you are asleep or at the beach.

Cross-promote and maintain branding across social media

Social media is one of the most powerful tools to build your brand and you must consider the full picture when you set up your business accounts. If you use the same name or handle on each account you set up, your customers will be able to find you much easier and connect with you on every channel. Make sure your handle or name is easy to remember and easily available on every platform you are active on.

Cross-promotion of all your social media accounts is important too, to enable your audience to connect with you in as many places as possible. If someone is following you on Twitter for example, they may not be connected to you on Facebook and this might be the network they prefer. All you need to do is send out a tweet that asks people to connect with your business on Facebook – make sure you follow up with a post that they can engage with and you stand a better chance of getting that all-important conversion.

Learn How to Start An Online Business For FREE:
www.lacobizonlinebusiness.com

Motivation

It's hard not to find some motivation when you read about all the successful online businesses, the riches and the satisfaction that people have gained but how long can you hold onto that motivation once you start your own business? Success is not guaranteed, not by a long shot and not everyone will be able to attain it. For others, there are rough seas ahead and, with success seeming to take so long to arrive, motivation can drain away very quickly.

If this sounds like you, I must warn you now – if you let feelings of hopelessness rule you, you will throw the towel in without giving your business the time it needs to succeed. You cannot expect success to appear after just a few days or weeks working at things and when you throw it in earlier, you will never know if the next day could have been the one that made you.

That said, it can be hard to remain motivated and to keep your thoughts positive so here are ten tips to help you.

Motivation Tip One – Make Sure Your Goals Are Achievable

Some new business owners have some very grand ideas and they set goals that are way beyond what they can achieve. All that does is set you up for disappointment. Yes, you need goals and yes, you need to set timelines and limits but they must be achievable and that means they have to be realistic. The easiest way to do it is this – set yourself one large major goal and then break it down into multiple smaller steps. Achieve those steps one at a time and within a reasonable time frame and each one will inspire you to move on, to maintain the motivation you need

Learn How to Start An Online Business For FREE: www.lacobizonlinebusiness.com

to keep on meeting those goals. One day, without you even realizing probably, you will have reached the end goal.

Motivation Tip Two – Maintain You're Dreams

When you first entered your business, you probably did it with the dream of great success, perhaps a year or so after you started. You may feel as though that dream is slipping out of your reach but that doesn't mean you should give up right away. Give yourself the time to answer this question – do you settle for nothing or do you keep working on the chance that success will be yours one day? I think it's an obvious answer.

Motivation Tip Three – Step Into Action

Look online and you will find a ton of information about starting an online business. Some of it will be useful, some won't. You will read how to do it, how to set up your marketing campaigns, how to do SEO, how to attract traffic, oh you will read everything. While reading is a good thing, you can do too much. And too much reading leads to too much overthinking and not enough action. Step into action quickly, while you read and learn because quick action can bring quick results and what better motivator is there than that?

Motivation Tip Four – Forecast Everything

Good business owners plan every last thing and they foresee every possible thing that can go wrong. If you are fully open to the fact that there will be failures along the way, you will find it much easier to rise back up and come up with another strategy to continue moving forward. Not only should you attempt to foresee what these failures may be, but you should also constantly monitor your passion. The only person who knows

Learn How to Start An Online Business For FREE:
www.lacobizonlinebusiness.com

you so well is you and only you know what is working and what isn't, whether your passion is waning or growing. If you think a business will bore you eventually, don't go into it; look for the business that will keep those flames burning.

Motivation Tip Five – Always Learn From Your Mistakes

Not one person in the world is perfect, although there are definitely those who think they are! When mistakes happen it is important that you do not beat yourself up over them. Mistakes are lessons in life and you should always learn from them so you don't make the same one again. Instead of berating yourself, find a solution to the problem and move forward.

Motivation Tip Six – Look for Real Inspiration

Inspiration is one of the keys to motivation so make sure you associate with those who are oriented by success and driven by passion. Their vibes will become yours and you can take your inspiration from their stories.

Motivation Tip Seven - Always Reward Yourself

Whenever you reach one of those goals you set, don't forget to reward yourself. You deserve that big pat on the back, after all, you put the work in to get there. Always credit yourself for the work you do and use it as your motivation to move on to the next step.

Motivation Tip Eight – Hold Yourself Accountable

Just because you are the boss of you, it doesn't mean that you are not going to be accountable to anyone else because you are. Your customers, for a start. You make them promises that you

Learn How to Start An Online Business For FREE: www.lacobizonlinebusiness.com

must keep. You made commitments that you cannot back out of. Always push forward and use every little success to keep you motivated to be accountable.

Motivation Tip Nine – Always Be Positive

Always look on the bright side of things. If you focus on negativity, your motivation will take a nosedive so push it to one side and keep positive at all times.

Motivation Tip Ten – Give Yourself a Break

When you first start your new business, the likelihood is you will work long hours without breaks for some time. Find a point where you can stop, where you can take a couple of days just to forget about it all and recharge. Take some time for you, refuel your drive and remember – motivation is not just about working all the hours you can; it's about balancing your life, fulfilling your dreams, and realizing that you did take the right step in starting your business after all.

Learn How to Start An Online Business For FREE: www.lacobizonlinebusiness.com

Press Outreach – 8 Mistakes to Avoid

Press outreach is quite possibly one of the biggest parts of your search engine optimization efforts and when you combine it with PR, or public relations, it can provide you with an incredibly effective way of gaining the right exposure for your online business in several places – not just on websites related to your industry but on some of the biggest media outlets. Do it right and you can reap huge rewards in terms of traffic to your website, great leads, plenty of sales, and links that you have earned.

I mentioned earlier about joining HARO to put yourself in the way of plenty of journalistic opportunities; remember, three emails are sent every day by HARO to their subscribers, each one filled with requests. There will be success for you here but only if you stick at it and you don't make these eight stupid mistakes.

Not Giving Enough Though To Your Pitch

When you receive one of these emails and it has a request in it that you think you can help with, you need to respond in the right way. Think about this way; if a journalist receives replies to their request within a minute then they can draw three conclusions:

- The responder has not given the response any thought at all

- The responder is replying to every single request. Nothing like throwing a load of BS at the wall and hoping that at least a little bit sticks

- Their response is not worth the time it takes to read it.

Learn How to Start An Online Business For FREE:
www.Iacobizonlinebusiness.com

What can you learn from this? Don't respond to every single request; very few of them will actually suit you. Instead, carefully choose one that you can respond to and then take the time to craft your response carefully. Work out how you can best help with the request, make your response helpful and intelligent. Not only will your insight stand a much better chance of being accepted and published, but you are also giving yourself the opportunity to get involved in a long-term relationship that can benefit your business in terms of exposure, not just now, but later on down the line too.

Not Checking Your Grammar

Poor grammar is a huge turn-off, especially from a journalistic point of view. You don't have to be a champion at spelling but do use the free grammar and spelling checks available to you. You could also have someone else look through it for you; a fresh eye can normally pick up on mistakes that you, the writer, misses. Another big no-no is text speak and social media slang. Yes, we all use it in our everyday lives but when you are touting for business, looking for exposure for your business, you do not use it. If you do, don't expect anyone to take you seriously.

Not Using a Professional Email Address

Where possible, do not use free email addresses such as Gmail, Hotmail or Yahoo of your business. It simply doesn't give a business-like impression. If you do have to use one of these for some reason, it is imperative that your email address is professional. Make sure it has your name in it, preferably your business name, and not some made-up name that looks totally unprofessional.

Learn How to Start An Online Business For FREE:
www.lacobizonlinebusiness.com

Seriously, if your personal email address has a name such as scoobeydoo@xxxx.com/co.uk, don't use it. At the very least, set up another email address that sounds more professional. It doesn't matter how good your response is; it could be the best of the bunch but, use an unprofessional email address and it won't even get looked at.

Using Copy and Paste Replies

These are spotted a mile off. The tone never sounds right and it won't answer the request properly which means it looks exactly like you never put any effort into it – which you didn't, of course. Your response has got to address the request, the questions that were asked in it.

Definitely do not use a copy and paste response that you already sent to another media outlet or contact. Most people who do this remember to change the name of the outlet they are responding to but there will always be that response that you forget to change and how unprofessional does that look! It's quite simple; if you can't take the time to write a proper response, don't bother.

Requesting a Link

When you write your response, never ever ask them to link back to your website as a reward for taking the time to respond to them. It screams that all you are interested in is yourself and not in helping out where you can. Provide the answer they want, provide the insight and the help they want and you will get that link without needing to ask for it.

Providing Incorrect Information

Learn How to Start An Online Business For FREE:
www.lacobizonlinebusiness.com

Don't start spouting data, facts and figures in your response without doing the research to back them up. These things change all the time and throwing around data that is clearly out of date will do you no good whatsoever. Also don't use technical jargon in the wrong place – it stands out that you don't really know what you are talking about. Quantity is a no-no here; quality all the way.

Chasing After the Wring Media Outlets

When you get the HARO emails, don't respond to requests to anything that do not relate to your industry. For example, let's say that you are in the web designing business. You shouldn't, then, respond to a request from a sports journalist. Media outreach is all about putting your business in front of the eyes of those who know your industry, who are likely to have an interest in it. Seriously, even if a sports website did mention you, you won't get any benefit from it; those who visit sports websites are not likely to be looking for someone to design a website for them.

Only respond to requests that you have proper experience in and you stand more chance of being accepted.

Writing a One-Sentence Response

Something along the lines of, "Hello, my advice to you would be ...." Is not going to get you anywhere. You waste your time writing it and they waste their time reading it and deleting it.

This kind of response indicates that you were busy doing something else when you saw the request and decided that you wanted to give it a go. The trouble is you don't really have the time right now so instead of setting aside time and doing it

Learn How to Start An Online Business For FREE: www.lacobizonlinebusiness.com

properly, you simply fire off a one-sentence reply. That is the biggest mistake you can make; that journalist will likely never look at your response again, no matter how good it is in the future.

Set aside an amount of time every day to deal with outreach matters and do it when you don't have anything else on the go. Too many hats will get in the way; effort is required to be a success.

Learn How to Start An Online Business For FREE:
www.␣lacobizonlinebusiness.com

Don't Sink Your Business This Quickly

Running a business is not easy but you can't cut corners. I heard of a man who was involved in marketing for his company; he thought he could change the numbers so they looked good but he ended up costing his company big money and losing his job as well. There are others who are too afraid to even think about trying something new, let alone take the jump. Those companies will be blown away by their competition, other companies who are prepared to take risks and get creative; companies who won't have to lay off their staff in the near future.

Marketing strategies are the life force of any company; get it wrong, your life force will die but get it right and you can live long into the future. These are the biggest marketing mistakes that can sink your business quicker than you can blink:

Sticking with old and ignoring the new

If there is one thing that is true about marketing, it's that it is an ever-changing landscape. As such it is your job, or the job of your marketing team, to stay on top of the latest trends in your industry. Yes, it is going to be far easier to focus your efforts on what you are doing now because it probably works. The trouble is, it won't work forever and if you don't keep up with the changes, you will be left behind incredibly quickly, possibly overtaken by newer businesses than yours because they took the time to get to know the new trends, to read the latest research and try out the newest tools. In simple terms, if you don't innovate, you go no further.

The first thing you should do is start each new business quarter with a completely new competitive analysis. Look at your nearest competitors; what are they doing that works that you are

Learn How to Start An Online Business For FREE: www.lacobizonlinebusiness.com

not doing? Have they been using social media more than you? Now who your competitors are and make use of the channels that are working for them – they may not all work for you but if you don't try, you won't know.

The next thing to do is speak to your vendors. You should really pencil in 2 days a year, spread apart, for marketing conferences. Make sure all your current vendors are invited as well as those who have tried to reach out to you and ask them all to come up with a pitch on what's happening and what's not – no more than 30 minutes each.

Lastly, research, research, research some more. Set aside time to research marketing websites and read all the latest information.

By doing all of this, you will have a constant stream of new ideas and you should set a portion of your yearly budget to one side to try some of them out. Aim for 10% of your budget; enough to give things a fair shot, not too much to make a difference if things don't work out.

Not attempting any growth hacks

A good growth hack can push your business ahead; a truly innovative one can send it spinning to the next level. In simple terms, a growth hack is nothing more than making the best and most creative use of available technology to expand your brand. If you do this right and come up with a working strategy, your business can be turned from a real struggle to a name on everyone's lips. Sadly, most marketers don't even think about it, let alone try it.

Much of the time this is down to a lack of creativity and time. We all know that running a business requires you to concentrate

Learn How to Start An Online Business For FREE: www.lacobizonlinebusiness.com

on every aspect, and much of your time will be taken analyzing your stats and data, checking your current channels for marketing and making sure your latest campaign is working; you still need to make time to come up with creative and innovative ways to use technology to market your business.

Make that time. Shut the door, switch off the phone, and turn off your computer. Close your eyes and think about how technology can be used to help you reach your audience. If you really can't think of anything, set up a brainstorming session with staff geeks who might just have a little more insight than you do and will likely be able to come up with a few solutions for you.

Quitting a campaign far too early

It's no secret that marketing a business can be quite expensive and time-consuming and that is why both time and money need to be invested if you are to make a sound decision of whether a campaign is working or not.

Take SEO, or search engine optimization, for example. This takes time for the results to be seen so, on all honesty, once you start an SEO campaign you should not even consider stopping it until it has been running for at least four months. In fact, don't even look for the results for that long. Competition is on the rise every day, especially in search engines like Google and expecting to sign up and be the top three of the page rankings immediately is simply not realistic. CRO or conversation rate optimization also takes quite a bit of time to achieve, several months in some cases before a new strategy can be converted based on what tests you have carried out.

Regardless of what you are doing, of what campaigns you are running, you need to fully understand the timeframe you are

Learn How to Start An Online Business For FREE: www.lacobizonlinebusiness.com

looking at before you sign up to it. Give your campaigns and the services you sign up to time to work before you consider pulling them. Don't expect immediate results because you won't get them. Give them time and the rewards will soon become self-evident.

Believing everything you hear

Every human being can be persuaded to do something, some more so than others. And there are very clever salespeople who learn all the dirty and underhand tactics to draw those people in and persuade them to sign up to something that won't work. When you decide to buy into a new service, don't believe everything the sales rep tells you. Do your own homework, your own analysis first. Your first place to look is Google. Good or bad, you will find all the information you want about a service. If you can't find any information you don't want the service.

Make sure you read the reviews, the good and the bad ones. Forget the company website; the testimonies are likely bought and paid for and probably are not genuine. You can validate this by attempting to contact the people who supposedly gave good reviews. Instead of believing what the website tells you, look for your own numbers that show you how the service performs. Lastly, check out the competition in the same way. You might find that the service you are being offered now can be bought through another company with a much better reputation and at a better price.

Whichever way you do it, do it. Don't take everything you hear for granted.

Trying to ignore the bad numbers

Learn How to Start An Online Business For FREE: www.lacobizonlinebusiness.com

Never see only what you want to see. Not all of your ideas will work, no matter how great or creative you think they are. Sometimes, that fantastic marketing campaign you dreamed up is nothing more than a flop.

You should always see things clearly. Don't be biased when you start to evaluate the numbers. If they tell you clearly that your plan just isn't working out then you need to be prepared to pull it and come up with a different one, even if it was the first plan you thought of. Let's assume that you have decided to set $20,000 aside to invest in a brand new ad network. Sadly, you don't see the revenue that you thought it would bring you. At this point, you need to be clear and you need to let the rest of your company now that it isn't working and you need to move on with something else. Don't try to highlight what isn't important in the hopes that the real numbers will go away.

The bottom line is this – don't attempt to make something look better than it is; if the situation is bad, accept it and put your resources where they will do the most good and bring you the most benefit.

You don't draw up a decent marketing plan

Whether you are in the business alone or you have others working for or with you, you still need a marketing plan. And that plan has to be exceedingly well organized and presented to everyone who works with or for you. There are loads of free templates online to help you with this, just run a quick Google search. While you do that, there are some general tips that you should take note of when you write your plan:

Always include a full timeline in your plan and a complete events calendar. Why should you do this? Because that is your

Learn How to Start An Online Business For FREE: www.lacobizonlinebusiness.com

way of setting the realistic expectation that you won't see results immediately and is a way of keeping your attention focused on the primary promotions that you have coming up. You will need to talk to other company members though and convince them that it is going to take time for your efforts to be realized into something good.

Make sure that each of your marketing initiatives is segmented out. And when you do this, you should also show the expected return on investment or ROI, and how you expect growth to be over a period of time. You should show a combination of projections – the low, the medium and the high ones.

Always have a contingency plan built in. You've heard the saying, "the best-laid plans of mice and men"; well. It's true. Not every plan is going to work and if something can go wrong, it will. At least that's how you should plan. Always have another plan in place should the first one come off the rails.

Failing to draw up a plan and including all the expectations and alternatives could mean the failure of your business. You won't be prepared for unexpected turns and you won't have done any of the strategic planning that you need to do to take your business on a level. Never expect everything to go right without making a plan to work by.

Not knowing what your core business model is

This is important stuff for any business and all business marketers need to know the following as an absolutely basic requirement:

- What the average value is of your customers

Learn How to Start An Online Business For FREE: www.lacobizonlinebusiness.com

- What length of time will your customers spend with you in total before they find another business?

- What profit does each customer bring you?

- How much are you aiming to spend to bring in each new customer and do you have any leeway on that cost?

- When your busiest times are and your slowest ones

- What your goals are for growth

- What your budget is. Do you have any amount of flexibility with it or is it set in stone?

- What makes a good customer? A bad one?

- What marketing channels you are using, how much each cost to run and what the return is for each channel.

Before any business owner can come up with a proper marketing strategy for their brand, they must have a full understanding of what the core business model is. By this, we are talking mostly about the numbers and, in a smaller way, the business subtleties. If you don't know this, you have no way of making any real decisions, let alone intelligent ones, for each of your chosen marketing channels.

Before you can even think about putting your strategy down on paper, understand all those core questions and the answers thoroughly. Learn as much about marketing as you can, all the general information you can, such as what personality does your business have? What values does your business hold and work by? What the personas of your major customers? What features

Learn How to Start An Online Business For FREE:
www.lacobizonlinebusiness.com

does your brand have that set it apart from your competitors? Do you know what your USP or unique selling proposition is?

Make sure you have all that information to hand before you even think about your strategy. Then, and only then, can you come up with a strategy that is aligned with your business model. That is the only way that you can truly maximize your full potential and revenue opportunities. Many business owners have no idea what these figures even mean, let alone have the answers to them and if you don't know the answers there is no way you can spend your budget in an effective and efficient way – the easiest way to damage the bottom line of your business without even trying.

It is so easy to sit here and write about the mistakes that you shouldn't make but here's the thing – it should be easy for you to avoid making them. Sadly many businesses flounder because they make these basic mistakes and it could all have been avoided with proper planning, creativity and alternatives to hand for when things go wrong – which they will.

Always be on top of the latest news and trends, be prepared to try out the latest tools and methods, make sure you know your numbers inside out and keep on top of them and, above all, be honest, with yourself and your customers. That's the only way to ensure your business can be successful and turn a profit.

Learn How to Start An Online Business For FREE:
www.lacobizonlinebusiness.com

Conclusion

Thank you again for downloading this book!

I hope this book was able to help you to understand exactly what is involved in setting up and running an online business. As you can see, it isn't a five-minute job and it isn't something you can do without any real effort. Most online businesses require some sort of financial outlay, even if it is just for setting up a website to run your business from.

However, if you are prepared to put the time and effort in, you can start to see money coming in fairly quickly. As with any job though, keeping at it is important to keep the bank balance growing! There are some basic tips that you should work to though:

- Be fully organized. That way you can stay on top of all your tasks and get them done in a timely fashion

- Keep records, detailed ones, right from day one

- Watch the competition and learn from them

- Understand what the risks are and what rewards you can reap by not being afraid to take some

- Be creative and always keep looking for ways that your business can be improved

- Maintain your focus; you won't be an immediate success but if you put the time in and keep your focus on your goals, success will come to you eventually

Learn How to Start An Online Business For FREE: www.lacobizonlinebusiness.com

- Be prepared to make a few sacrifices, mostly time sacrifices, at least to start with

- Provide the best service you possibly can and strive to make it better

- Consistency is key – keep doing what you have to do if you want to be successful.

The next step is to get yourself set up! Choose your business model, after weighing up the pros and cons of each one, set your website up and go for it. If you don't try, you will always be that person on the sideline, spending your life wishing you had taken the leap. Take that leap and change your life forever. It won't be easy but it will be rewarding, that much I can promise you.

Finally, if you enjoyed this book, then I'd like to ask you for a favor, would you be kind enough to leave a review for this book on Amazon? It'd be greatly appreciated!

Thank you and good luck!

Learn How to Start An Online Business For FREE:
www.lacobizonlinebusiness.com

Made in the USA
Monee, IL
08 March 2023